THE TRUEST STORY EVER TOLD

WHAT THE WORLD'S MOST TIMELESS STORIES REVEAL ABOUT FINDING FULFILLMENT, JOY AND ADVENTURE

MICHAEL B. EDDY

PUBLISHED BY

WHOLEHEARTED

Published by Wholehearted Media
Atlanta, GA

Scripture quotations noted NIV are from the HOLY BIBLE: NEW INTERNATIONAL VERSION®. Copyright © 1973, 1978, 1984 by International Bible Society.

ISBN: 978-0-692-17188-2

Book layout by www.ebooklaunch.com

To my little heroes:

Brooks, Wade and Millie

CONTENTS

PART I

CHAPTER I

WIRED FOR STORY

IN THE 1940S A PAIR OF PSYCHOLOGISTS named Fritz Heider and Marianne Simmel constructed an animated film starring a small triangle, a large triangle, and a circle. For two and half minutes, the shapes moved around a colorless background at varying speeds and direction. As an experiment Heider and Simmel showed the film to thirty-five college students and asked them to describe what they had seen. Only one student described the scene as geometric shapes in motion. The other thirty-four students perceived far more than two triangles and a circle made of cardboard. From this rudimentary animation the students constructed elaborate stories. These weren't just shapes colliding on a flat plane; this was high drama. If you looked closely enough, you might see a story of unrequited love or an underdog up against a sinister force. These shapes experienced conflict and resolution; some were villains, and others were heroines. The shapes' lack of dimension and color didn't restrain the students' imagination. Closer examination revealed that these shapes experienced emotions such as loneliness, pain, jealousy and anger. At least this is how the students who watched the film reported what they saw.[1]

You can go to YouTube today and try this experiment for yourself.[2] It has been repeated many times with the same results. Most people will see the geometric shapes in motion and without even a conscious awareness break into spontaneous storytelling in their minds. Before they know it, they are cheering for a triangle, feeling sympathy for a circle or sweating about whether the small triangle will prevail over the big one.

This is human nature; we are storytelling creatures. Stories differentiate us from the rest of the animal kingdom. For example, animals don't bury their dead because they don't have a story for what happens after death. Humans do, which is why burial ceremonies characterize every human society dating back to at least to the Paleolithic era 30,000 years ago.[3] If we didn't have a story about what happens when a person dies, why would we bother? Of course, stories aren't limited to explanations of the afterlife. From the beginning storytelling has helped man sort out his relationship to his environment and to his community, and has served as instructive wisdom on what life on this planet is about.

How long have humans been telling stories? It's hard to say for sure, but an accidental discovery in 1994 by three spelunkers exploring a limestone mountain range in south-central France revealed that this storytelling feature of man is no modern advance. Hiking along the ridge of one of the whitewashed cliffs near Toulouse, France, the three friends detected a slight updraft of cool air coming from a recess along the ledge. They heaved rocks away until they could squeeze themselves through a small opening that led to an entrance of a deep shaft descending into the mountain. Prepared for a day of cave exploration, they unfurled a chain ladder and continued thirty feet downward through the cramped passage until they came to a "soaring grotto with a domed roof."[4] Suddenly, they stood in one of the many rooms that make up what archeologists now call the Chauvet Cave (so named for one of the three French adventurers who discovered it). It didn't take them long to realize this was no ordinary cave. This was history, and a normal day of cave exploration had turned into an epic discovery. Lit by their headlamps, they gazed upon a trove of ancient artwork. They were the first humans to explore the exquisite artistry within the cave since a landslide had sealed it away thousands of years earlier.

The walls of Chauvet Cave contain over 1,000 painted art scenes dating as far back as 37,000 years ago. According to carbon recordings, new scenes were added to the original paintings during various millennia, with some artwork being a young age of only 10,000 years! When I first read about the art found in Chauvet Cave, I had a picture in my mind of rudimentary paintings, at best. I imagined stick figures etched into the stone pursuing a geometrical shape that archaeologists would claim to be a wooly mammoth. The invention of writing is marked as beginning around 3,200 BC with the emergence of a wedge-shaped alphabet known as cuneiform.[5] The images in Chauvet Cave were made 35,000 years before that. Imagination and artistic skill aside, I wondered how well someone could paint on a rock canvas with whatever blunt tools that a person living 37,000 years ago might have used to leave his artistic mark.

What I learned is we should not underestimate the artistic sense of prehistoric humans! Reporter Judith Thurman writing for the *New Yorker* magazine visited the caves in 2007. Here is her description of the skill and inventiveness she discovered in the scenes captured on the walls of the lost cave:

> *What those first artists invented was a language of signs for which there will never be a Rosetta stone; perspective, a technique that was not rediscovered until the Athenian Golden Age; and a bestiary of such vitality and finesse that, by the flicker of torch-light, the animals seem to surge from the walls, and move across them like figures in a magic lantern show (in that sense, the artists invented animation). They also thought up the grease lamp—a lump of fat, with a plant wick, placed in a hollow stone—to light their workplace; scaffolds to reach high places; the principles of stenciling and Pointillism; powdered colors, brushes, and stumping cloths.* [6]

What were these talented prehistoric artists doing in these caves? Why did they go through the trouble of building scaffolding to extend their art to the unreachable places on a wall? What motivated them to paint in exquisite detail a frieze of horse profiles? What inspired them to adopt techniques that art historians have credited to cultures that came tens of thousands of years later? They were storytelling. Man has never lived without his innate sense for the drama unfolding in the world around him. And the desire to share those stories with his community and inform the generations to come is universal.

One of the leading archeology scholars in the study of the Chauvet Cave claims, "Everyone agrees that the paintings are, in some way, religious. I'm not a believer myself, and I'm certainly not a mystic. But *Homo sapiens* is *Homo spiritualis*. The ability to make tools defines us less than the need to create belief systems that influence nature."[7] In this cave we get a rare glimpse into the mind of our ancient ancestors, and what is it we discover? They are just like us. Where we thought we would discover clues about the perfunctory tools and patterns of life required to survive in a prehistoric world, we find a deeper mystical revelation. They went to the cave on a spiritual journey. Their life is no more defined by stone weapons and fire than ours is by computers and automobiles. We are connected more than we know. What they sought is what we seek 37,000 years later: an explanation for our place in the cosmos. What did our ancestors experience in those caves? A captivating and immortal story—a vision quest for clues about how to live the good life.

While history suggests storytelling is an inherited trait hardwired in all of us, you don't have to stumble upon cave art from thousands of years ago to know this is true. You can simply observe any young child at play. Children live in stories. When they imagine the world, which children do constantly, they are creating stories. It doesn't take long for them to reason out universal themes. The stories often include good versus evil, a hero and a villain and conflict that must be resolved. I have three children aged ten, eight and four as of this writing, and they all seem to know what the important elements of a story are with no instruction on the subject.

Our neighbors remain unaware of this, but the woods by our house are an enchanted forest full of magical beasts and dangerous robbers to defeat. The playground set in our backyard may seem ordinary with its requisite swings and slide, but it's actually a concealed space station for intrepid space rangers. Our basement is a royal court whence great adventures and battles may be launched on a rainy weekend. I have confirmed that my children aren't crazy by quizzing their friends, and they also recognize that these stories are taking place.

No doubt my children would create their own narratives for the triangles and circle in the Heider-Simmel animation. They don't require instructions on how to create a story. They inherited the trait. And storytelling is neither something we engage in occasionally nor a domain reserved only for children. We spend our entire lives engrossed in them. Jonathan Gottschall, author of the book *Storytelling Animal*, points out that humans are addicted. "Even when the body goes to sleep, the mind stays up all night, telling itself stories."[8] They come so readily that we may not even be aware how much they direct our thoughts. Without stories the world would remain an ambiguous blob of data and facts, hard to process and difficult to find meaning in.

The Curious Case of Language

Gottschall refers to man as *Homo fictus*, "the great ape with a storytelling mind."[9] This development, though, in our species is truly extraordinary. We have already pointed out that stories distinguish us from the rest of the animal kingdom. But it's hard to overstate how remarkable and incomprehensible this gap is. It is no small evolutionary leap to become a storytelling animal. The mental and anatomical tools required to develop language alone, much less conceive of stories using that language, is a confounding development for scientists.

Neuroscientist Stephen Pinker summed this idea up in his book, *The Language of Instinct: The New Science of Language and Mind*:

> *As you are reading these words, you are taking part in one of the wonders of the natural world. For you and I belong to a species with a remarkable ability: we can shape events in each other's brains with remarkable precision. I am not referring to telepathy or mind control or the other obsessions of fringe science; even in the depictions of believers, these are blunt instruments compared to an ability that is uncontroversially present in every one of us. That ability is language. Simply by making noises with our mouths, we can reliably cause precise new combinations of ideas to arise in each other's minds. The ability comes so naturally that we are apt to forget what a miracle it is..... Human language is based on a very different design..... Even the seat of human language in the brain is special.....* [10]

Philosopher Bertrand Russell put it more succinctly: "A dog cannot relate his autobiography; however eloquently he may bark, he cannot tell you that his parents were honest though poor." Furthermore, the whole idea of language is a problem for evolutionary biologists. For many reasons its presence does not fit their models. This may explain why Pinker in the preceding quote refers to this phenomenon as a "miracle," not the term you would expect an evolutionary scientist to use in describing human design, but perhaps not inaccurate either.

Renowned linguistic scholar Noam Chomsky says, "Human language appears to be a unique phenomenon, without significant analogue in the animal world..... There is no reason to suppose that the 'gaps' are bridgeable. There is no more of a basis for assuming an evolutionary development from breathing to walking." [11]

For some time philosophers and scientists have argued that language is learned through environment. The evidence of more recent study suggests that language is fundamental to the human makeup. Chomsky believes that all humans share a "Universal Grammar," a language organ which pre-programs every person with the blueprint to understand language. We may learn a particular language based on where we grow up and the language our parents speak, but our ability to grasp that language is a peculiar and innate ability—one that is particular to the human species alone.

For some time biologists have wondered why no animal species have developed at least some simple nouns, verbs or sentence structures. We know other animals have sophisticated reasoning and intelligence skills. A group of scientists once taught a chimpanzee to play the video game Pac-Man and to use a keyboard to communicate basic needs. Other animals use sophisticated social cues as well, but this is far different from what we would define as language.

Furthermore, it's not that scientists haven't tried to teach other animals language. There have been numerous studies performed by PhDs who were confident that certain intelligent animals could be taught language if they only had the right environment for learning. Two conclusions can be reached from these experiments: either PhDs make lousy language instructors or apes and chimpanzees are dull language learners. It's not that the PhDs completely failed their primate pupils; it's just that, compared to the average two-year-old human, the rate of language acquisition in the animal world seems rather slow and unsophisticated.

This led another evolutionary biologist, Terrence Deacon, in his book, *The Symbolic Species: The Co-evolution of Language and the Brain,* to conclude, "Biologically, we are just another ape. Mentally, we are a new phylum of organisms." Despite all of the advances in neuroscience, biology and archeology, this remains an enormous mystery to those who work from an assumption that evolution alone can explain man (and every one of his attributes). Deacon goes on to say, "In this context, then, consider the case of human language. It is one of the most distinctive behavioral adaptations on the planet. Languages evolved in only one species, in only one way, without precedent, except in the most general sense. And the differences between languages and all other natural modes of communicating are vast."[12]

The reason this distinction is important is because language is far more than communication. It's an entirely different mode of thinking. It is the ability to make symbolic representations. This is what makes *homo sapiens'* communication so fundamentally different from any other species' communication. Animals don't tell stories because they can't think in terms of symbolic representations.

An Alternative Theory

Philosopher, linguist and author Owen Barfield argued that language and myth (our oldest stories) are interlocked and inseparable. Myth describes humankind's perceptions of its relationship to the world, and language emerged as a vehicle of expression for those concepts. According to Barfield, language doesn't enable stories (i.e., myths); it exists because of stories. Barfield points out how languages begin with figurative words and only later evolve into more specific and literal meanings. "As we go back in history language becomes more picturesque, until its infancy, when it is all poetry; or all spiritual facts are represented by natural symbols."[13] Man was a poet first, and language exists because of man's desire to express inner meaning.

Scientists have no clear answers as to when, where, why or how man became a storytelling animal. Investigation of some of these troubling questions surrounding the storytelling man lead to more confounding questions. These questions and the theories that go along with them are well beyond the scope of this book and the academic credentials of this author. What I want to highlight is that the skill of symbolic reference, which enables language and storytelling, is an amazing and unexpected outcome, so much so that a rigorous evolutionary scientist might even use the word *miracle* to describe it. If we want to understand our unique design as humans, the skill set of symbolic representation, mankind's capacity and tendency to live by stories, seems an excellent starting point.

More importantly, perhaps design reveals something about the intent of the designer. If you happened to believe in a divine creator, you might look at this particular piece of engineering as a starting point for better understanding the designer's purpose. Science has a principle known as Occam's razor, which specifies that when there are multiple competing theories, the simplest theory should be preferred to the more complex theory. Perhaps the simplest explanation for the miracle of the storytelling animal is one that can be found in a short tale told by Elie Wiesel in the introduction to his book, *Gates of the Forest.*

Wiesel's story is about a series of Hasidic leaders who must each follow a three-part ritual to save his community from disaster. The ritual tradition calls for each rabbi to perform three steps: (1) to find a specific place in the forest, (2) to light a fire there and (3) to recite a specific prayer. Each rabbi goes out and follows the three steps, and each time the community is saved, but with each rabbi, one of the rituals is forgotten until we come to the fourth rabbi:

> *The years passed. And it fell to Rabbi Israel of Ryzhyn to over-come misfortune. Sitting in his armchair, his head in his hands, he spoke to God: "I am unable to light the fire, and I do not know the prayer, and I cannot even find the place in the forest. All I can do is tell the story, and this must be sufficient." And it was sufficient.*
>
> *God made man because he loves stories.*[14]

This reminds me of the first three words in the Bible: "In the beginning...." From the outset, the entire Bible is framed as a story with a classic opening. The Author of the Universe sets the scene. He speaks and light appears for the first time. He follows that with the sky and heavens. Next, he creates the stars and moon in the night sky. He gathers water into the great oceans, and from those waters rise the land. Each day he adds to the stage he is building. He fills the waters with the great creatures of the sea and the land with all other living creatures. The Bible says he completes this work in five days and then on the sixth day he adds his final touch:

> *So God created mankind in his own image,*
> *in the image of God he created them;*
> *male and female he created them.* (Gen. 1:27 NIV)

In other words, the Author of the Universe builds a global theater, a stage of endless possibilities, a backdrop of immense beauty and diversity. Then he sets down his actors, each bearing his image, into the unfolding drama of earth and humanity. Perhaps the reason we humans have always been captivated by stories is because we were made to participate in the eternal story that began with our creation. We can't escape our design.

Why Humans Need Stories

Whatever you believe about creation, there is no denying how much of life is consumed in stories. When we convene with friends and families, we spend much of that time telling stories about ourselves or gossiping (telling stories about others). The average American adult spends over five hours a day watching television, which is about 30 percent of waking hours.[15] I believe our innate attraction to stories is the reason for the strong appeal of sports in our society. Each match is a tale of good guys against bad guys and an invitation to become invested in our heroes and their conflict. Even when we seek a break from all the media clamoring for our attention, commercial stories bombard us during the match, and it's no secret that the most effective commercial messages make us feel as though we could be the hero of the story if we only had that car or those shoes.

Without a doubt stories entertain us and inform us, but they have a far more important role than to provide information and recreation. The best stories are self-reflections. The stories that captivate us most aren't just about the people on a screen or the characters on a page. They are about us. The important stories shine a mirror into our souls and beg us for examination. Our imagination is always practicing and preparing for its own tests and trials. It's not content to be a passive participant. It wants to be part of the action. "Stories train *implicit* memories—the knowledge you have without knowing that you know it. In other words, *Hamlet*'s draw isn't that it will give you good tips on handling your struggle to run Denmark, but rather that it will give you three hours' more practice at empathizing with others, judging their actions and evaluating their motives. You won't remember the specifics, any more than you recall how you learned to ride a bike, but the practice, like all practice, will help.[16]

When we become captured by a story, we intuit the emotions of the characters we are watching or reading about, a term cognitive scientists call "transportation." We feel joy when the protagonist reaches his or her dreams even though we know the protagonist's ascension is fiction. We know the star actor doesn't love the star actress, but we feel sorrow when she leaves him in the movie. Stories have a remarkable way of breaking through our intellectual defenses. Jonathan Gottschall goes on to say, "Fiction seems to be more effective at changing beliefs than nonfiction, which is designed to persuade through argument and evidence. Studies show that when we read nonfiction, we read with our shields up. We are critical and skeptical. But when we are absorbed in a story, we drop our intellectual guard. We are moved emotionally, and this seems to make us rubbery and easy to shape."[17]

Stories are a training ground for living, and the best ones provide important instruction and inspiration. But others' stories shouldn't replace the act of living our own. The truth we seek and the transformation we each need cannot be accomplished for us. They can only be achieved by engaging in the unfolding drama of our very own life. Great books, movies, plays and music are beautiful gifts to be enjoyed and relished, but they will betray us if we ask them to do too much. We cannot find life and purpose through them; they are only signposts beckoning us toward our own authorship.

In the pages to come, we will explore how a certain personal story provides the context we all need to make sense of life. There is a reason stories have been so intertwined in the history and special architecture of our species. God made man because he loves stories. And as we shall see, not any story can serve as our guide. What we need is the timeless wisdom and character of a certain genre of storytelling. In the next chapter we will turn our attention to a framework that has stood the test of time and in its various expressions in history has always informed man and the community on what it means to live in accordance with the universe.

If we could come to understand our lives through the universal themes of the mythmakers, they would reveal much about what is happening in the world and what life expects from us next. As members of a modern scientific community, it's tempting for us to discount the wisdom of myth, but this is a mistake. Comparative religion scholar Karen Armstrong explains: "Like science and technology, mythology, as we shall see, is not about opting out of this world, but about enabling us to live more intensely within it."[18] Life could be more than an endless to-do list of appointments, obligations and deadlines that dominate modern life. But for most of us, our day-to-day existence couldn't feel farther from any kind of mythical quest. The reason for this is that we need a better filter and a more powerful guide.

For too many of us, our lives ceased having any notion of a meaningful story long ago. Life hasn't delivered what we used to imagine when we were naive enough to really imagine things for our lives. So we separate the story from our reality and try to content ourselves by escaping for a night at the movies or a good book by the fire.

Finding the Right Context

Mythologist Joseph Campbell observed that "life is like arriving late for a movie, having to figure out what is going on without bothering everybody with a lot of questions, and then being unexpectedly called away before you find out how it ends." We don't know why we are here; the plot of life is elusive and ends abruptly before most of us understand the point of it. But our interpretation of things depends on our filter and expectations. Is life about getting by, "working for the man," saving for retirement and just surviving? Are the only certainties death and taxes?

If you look closer, you may find in the midst of the chaos that there is an amazing drama unfolding and that you have an opportunity to become a part of the grand narrative being told about the world. But first you must choose your filter of interpretation. You may either remain a passive member of the audience or take your place on the stage. The suffering of life can rule, or you can find beauty in the midst of it. You may become discouraged by the banality of the flesh or find reason for hope. You can be embittered by the mundane of daily living or discover adventure. Life can dictate the narrative, or you can write your own tale.

Sixteen hundred years ago, St Augustine wrote, "Men go abroad to admire the heights of mountains, the mighty waves of the sea, the broad tides of rivers, the compass of the ocean, and the circuit of the stars, yet pass over the mystery of themselves without a thought." The answers we all seek and the context we all need is written onto the human heart and memorialized in our great stories. That's why the best stories have such an impact. They remind us of our deepest desires, and they light the way toward self-discovery. All of us have our own set of circumstances and our own journey to make, but we don't have to make the journey alone. The pattern of the story has remained the same for millennia. The requirements are the same, too; from the cave painter peering through the dim light of his plant wick 37,000 years ago to the businessperson peering through the dim light of a computer screen, "we have only to follow the thread of the hero-path," said Joseph Campbell - a particular story framework that has informed every human culture in history.

You may not realize it, but you already know this story's blueprint. Its appeal is universal, and so is its application. Even in modern society, it's impossible to go a day without encountering the Hero's Journey in a book, song, movie, television show or just about any other media in which a story can be shared. What is this Hero's Journey? And how does it allow us to live more intensely in the world? These are the questions we will address in the next chapter.

CHAPTER II

HERO'S JOURNEY

IN 1973 A YOUNG FILMMAKER IN CALIFORNIA worked his way through most of the Hollywood movie studios pitching a new idea. He carried with him a thirteen-page outline of a vision for a film that he had been dreaming up for two years. He wanted to create in his own words a modern-day fairy tale, but he struggled to convince the movie executives of his vision, and he was politely dismissed by them all.

Although the filmmaker had completed the filming of his debut movie earlier in the year, the studio that owned the distribution rights had not released it to theaters. The filmmaker had no track record of success and no income. The poor, starving artist wondered if he would make it in the film business. But he kept pitching his idea to anyone who would listen until one day a friend in the industry offered him a $15,000 advance to turn his thirteen-page outline into a Hollywood-ready screenplay. It wasn't a lot of money, but it was enough to keep his dream alive. At least for the time being he wouldn't have to wait tables to pay his rent.

As the filmmaker conceived of the plot for his movie, he reflected that modern society no longer had a common mythology. In his words society was losing "the type of stories we tell our children," which was an important medium "for how our heritage gets passed from one generation to the next." Old Western movies had attempted to bring mythology to American culture, but by the 1970s Western movies had fallen out of fashion. The filmmaker asked himself where the culture could turn next to develop a modern mythology? He noticed that

16

myth often came from the "borders of society, from out there, from places of mystery."

By the 1970s humans had explored most of earth but were just beginning to explore outer space. It was only a few years earlier that Buzz Aldrin's voice had come crackling through the living room television sets and radios of America, announcing his departure from the Apollo Lunar landing module onto the surface of the moon. Since then space had captured America's imagination. It was a place of great mystery but also of inspiration, bringing a sense of wonder and awe about creation and what might lie beyond our own orbit. The filmmaker decided space would be the appropriate setting for his modern-day fairy tale.

However, transforming his space-based fairy tale into a Hollywood-ready screenplay proved to be a daunting task. In his mind the filmmaker could visualize important scenes and motifs that he wanted to explore, but he lacked a coherent framework from which to hang his vision. He struggled to write, and month after month went by without a suitable product emerging from his efforts. One day, discouraged by his lack of progress, the filmmaker stumbled across a book he had read in college as part of his studies in anthropology. The book, entitled, "*A Hero with a Thousand Faces*," proved to be the missing input the filmmaker needed to complete his screenplay. Published in 1949 by a professor at Sarah Lawrence College in New York named Joseph Campbell, *A Hero with a Thousand Faces* outlined the mythological journey of heroic archetypes. The book helped give shape to the various themes that the filmmaker was trying to work out for his own myth. With the influence of Campbell's writing, the screenplay fell into place around a unique, coherent and strangely familiar narrative.

In 1976, almost three years after he began pitching his thirteen-page outline, a draft of the screenplay was completed. During the writing process, the filmmaker's first movie, *American Graffiti*, was finally released to widespread critical acclaim and was nominated for an Academy Award for Best Picture. The filmmaker was able to turn the success of his first movie into the financial support he needed to bring his ambitious new screenplay to life, and filming began shortly after the completion of the screenplay.

As the final version of the movie came together, the filmmaker screened a rough cut for a group of friends along with several movie executives and other Hollywood directors. Almost all of those attending the initial screening hated it. Some even openly mocked the film for its "comic-book characters, unbelievable story, lack of political or social commentary, lousy acting, preposterous dialogue, and a ridiculously simplistic morality."[1] His friends worried that the film would be a complete disaster and might ruin what could have been a promising career.

On edge before the movie's release to the public, the filmmaker decided he needed to get away from California, so he booked a trip to Hawaii to "hide out" during the movie's debut in theaters. He hoped the reception he received from his friends, movie executives and Hollywood directors wasn't a good predictor of the movie-going public. After a couple of days, he received a call from a friend back in California, urging him to turn on the evening news. He turned on the television, and the legendary news anchor, Walter Cronkite, came on the television saying, "There's something extraordinary happening out there, and it's all the result of a new movie called *Star Wars*." The news cut to a shot of a theater in Manhattan, where there was a line of people around the block people waiting to see the new space-based fairy tale.

The rest is movie history. George Lucas, the young filmmaker, had bottled magic. The *Star Wars* franchise would become the most successful movie franchise in history, grossing almost $9 billion in worldwide box office sales across its various titles, not to mention the collectibles, toys, theme parks, video games and countless other products spawned from the saga over the years. *Stars Wars* still enjoys a cultlike following today, and an entire generation came of age imagining themselves as part of the adventures taking place "a long time ago in a galaxy far, far away."[2] When Lucas later talked about the influence that Joseph Campbell had on the making of the movie, the rest of Hollywood took notice. George Lucas had become a household name and had changed the face of the movie industry overnight. Not surprisingly, others wondered what his recipe for success was. At one point Lucas admitted, "About 10 years ago I set out to do, had an idea of doing a modern fairy tale and stumbled across *Hero with a Thousand Faces*. After reading more of Joe's [Joseph Campbell's] books I began to understand how I could do this. It was a great gift ... and a very important moment. It's possible if I hadn't run across that I would still be writing *Star Wars* today."[3]

Inspired as a child by the myths of Native American culture, Campbell spent most of his life studying and comparing myths from around the world, hoping to understand humanity and its fascination with stories. One of his most important insights was to highlight a common thread running through all the myth traditions he studied. It didn't matter whether the story came from an ancient civilization or a medieval one. It didn't matter whether the myth came from a tribal group of the North American plains or one from the African Savannah. One theme always repeated itself throughout the history of mythology. Campbell referred to it as the "monomyth," or "Hero's Journey." By just reading the chapter titles of a *Hero with a Thousand Faces*, it's easy to discern the path Lucas took when we wrote *Star Wars*, with each chapter title of Campbell's book matching the key decisive events of the *Star Wars* saga.

Because of Lucas's success, the Hero's Journey framework quickly infiltrated the movie-making business. Studios used the Hero's Journey to analyze scripts and decide which ones to accept or reject. Directors and screenwriters internalized the framework to the point where without even realizing it, they could scarcely conceive of a story without using the structure of the Hero's Journey. Aspiring screenwriters attended workshops and read books on how to use the Hero's Journey in their creative process. One recent analysis identifies the Hero's Journey as the foundation for more than half of the movies that come out of Hollywood.[4]

The following is a small sample of well-known movies following the Hero's Journey framework: *The Wizard of Oz, Casablanca, The Lord of the Rings* trilogy, the *Harry Potter* series, *Gladiator, The Matrix, Fight Club, The Karate Kid, Jaws, Braveheart, Dances with Wolves, Spider-Man, Rocky, American Beauty, Finding Nemo,* and *The Lion King.* The list goes on and on, and as you read through the stages of the Hero's Journey, you will recognize its structure in other movies, plays and novels that you love.

The Hero's Journey works for a reason, and most great storytellers don't even need instruction on how to write about it. For example, *The Wizard of Oz*, *Casablanca* and *The Lord of the Rings* trilogy were all written before Joseph Campbell laid out his theory, and yet they follow the same pattern. The reason is that Campbell did not invent anything new. He simply chronicled the great stories told since the beginning of humanity. What he found is that they are all basically the same story repeated with endless variations.

The most persistent theme in both oral and written literature is the one in which "A hero ventures forth from the world of common day into a region of supernatural wonder; fabulous forces are there encountered and a decisive victory is won: the hero comes back from the mysterious adventure with the power to bestow boons on his fellow man."[5]

Great storytellers require neither instruction nor an outline such as Campbell's. The best ones are already attuned to what makes us human—our desires, fears and longings—and the stories they tell appeal to those traits. The universal nature of stories is a reflection of eternal truths. That's why they spring forth and repeat themselves without any coordination. It's also why they resonate so deeply with each of us. When we are not analyzing the story but, instead, are allowing it to enter into the deepest recesses of our soul, the story connects with something that goes beyond reason alone. We experience something beyond the words. We connect with ourselves and with the world in a way that is not easily articulated. Consequently, if we will allow ourselves a moment of freedom, we will find in the story of the Hero that there is something mythical about creation and life.

As part of an academic study, *A Hero with a Thousand Faces* is not the first place where this mythological phenomenon of the timeless Hero can be observed. Campbell's theory follows and builds on the work of others who made similar observations in the fields of anthropology, mythology and psychology. Campbell sometimes referred to the Hero's Journey as the "monomyth," a term he borrowed from his literary hero James Joyce, who is best known for his story of a modern-day Ulysses, the quintessential Greek and Roman hero. It is Joyce who first defined the monomyth as "a cyclical journey or quest undertaken by a mythical hero."

As modern anthropology developed at the beginning of the twentieth century, scholars such as James Frazer and Lord Ragland, among others, wrote about the strangely similar motifs they found in myths coming from vastly different cultural and environmental heritages. Christian writers and mythologists such as C. S. Lewis and J.R.R. Tolkien discuss the commonalities of myth in detail in their writings. Lewis, with *Chronicles of Narnia*, and Tolkien, with *The Lord of the Rings and The Hobbit*, were two of the most famous mythmakers of the twentieth century. Neither one of them knew Joseph Campbell, but both follow the Hero's Journey in their fictional writings.

In his study of mythology, Campbell tried to understand the deeper implications of these recurring themes, namely, what they say about human nature. For help in understanding this, Campbell cited the work of renowned Swiss psychiatrist and psychoanalyst, Carl Jung. Jung's research focused on *archetypes*, which can be defined as an original model on which other similar things are patterned. What interested Jung were the common symbols and themes that repeatedly appeared in the dreams of his clinical psychiatric patients. Jung observed that the archetypes of his patients' dreams had a strong correspondence to the common archetypes running through mythology.

Jung concluded that these recurring archetypes were evidence of some psychic element present in all human beings. He labeled this phenomenon the "collective unconscious." Jung believed that humans are born with an innate ability to recognize and imagine these common myths as a tool for playing out the drama of life. In other words, archetypes had an instinctual origin and were therefore critical to understanding human psychology. In deference to Jung's research, Campbell concluded that "myths are public dreams, dreams are private myths." [6] What Campbell meant is that mythological stories reveal something fundamental about human nature and consciousness.

This brings us back to the point I made in the first chapter about the inseparability of man and his stories, and how history and biology suggest that our species is unable to sustain itself in the world without them. What Campbell and others are suggesting is that mythology, as a particular means of storytelling, conveys important insights about what it means to be human. And while the Hero's Journey has proven to be a great tool for screenwriters, novelists and playwrights, it has a far more important implication regarding what life is expecting from us and how we can live more richly. It offers an invitation to experience our lives in the context of a meaningful and eternal story.

Outlining the Hero's Journey

Each Hero's Journey entails three main acts through which the Hero or (Heroine) travels: Departure, Initiation and Return. Broadly speaking, the Hero must "depart" from the comfortable and known world into a mysterious world of trials and challenges where he learns deep truths about himself and is "initiated" into a new kind of existence as he dies to his old ways of life. Once the Hero is initiated, he then "returns" to the world from which he set out, where he uses his newfound power and strength to help his fellow man. The phases of the journey should be thought of as a cyclical process, repeating themselves over and over again. After the Hero returns to bestow his gifts on his fellow man in his normal world, he is once again called out on a new adventure and the process begins anew. For our purposes, we will use "Hero" as a non-gender-specific term; just as a poet or a writer may mean a male or a female, so does "Hero" in the context of the rest of this manuscript.

Within the three major acts of departure, initiation and return, Campbell identified seventeen thematic structures, or sub-acts, through which the Hero passes during the journey. Over the next few pages, I will attempt, in my own words, to summarize the various sub-acts identified in Campbell's book, *A Hero with a Thousand Faces*. In Part II of the book we will examine these themes of the Hero's Journey in detail and discuss how they might be applied to our own lives. Before we continue, it's important to note that the Hero's Journey isn't a rigid prescription. Every journey has its own pace and nuances. The Hero isn't necessarily required to pass through every single one of the archetypal sub-acts in order to succeed. Sometimes the chronology of the various acts may shift. But while the specifics of each journey change, the same themes do repeat themselves within the three-part macro-cycle of departure, initiation and return. Above all, the universal Hero's Journey is simply the ongoing cycle of leaving his world to find the source of life in order to evolve into a richer or more mature human being.

Call to Adventure

The Hero's Journey begins with a Call to Adventure when some information is received that beckons the Hero to leave the mundane normalcy of his current surroundings and venture into the unknown. The call brings a new awareness to the Hero and draws him into a relationship with forces he doesn't quite understand. Sometimes the journey is introduced by a "Herald," a symbolic or literal figure summoning the Hero to look beyond his current circumstances and understanding about the world around him. In some cases the Hero is called to the adventure out of a crisis created by his own shortcomings or by the shortcomings of others. At other times he is enticed from the common path of life by some interesting phenomenon. Sometimes the Hero is set on his journey by the will of another. Often what the Hero values and cherishes begins to shift as he becomes aware that much of what he thinks is real is, in fact, an illusion. As the truth about reality becomes apparent, he becomes aware of a new destiny. The Hero quickly recognizes that the Call to Adventure will require much of him. It will require that he change, adapt and allow himself to be transfigured in order to accomplish his mission.

Refusal of the Call

The Hero has a choice right away: to answer the call or not. In many cases the Hero may turn away from the adventure. He may refuse out of duty and responsibility to his Ordinary World. Often he will feel reluctance out of fear or feelings of inadequacy. He may sense what lies beyond the pale and may not want to depart from the comforts of his surroundings and his way of life. And, though he may succeed in building upon his kingdom and comfortable way of life, his refusal to answer the call robs him of his power. By refusing the call, he may get what he wants but in getting it, he also becomes a victim. The life and the story that he wants to control, in the end, control him. Sometimes the Hero will initially refuse the call, but with further guidance or on further reflection, he may reconsider.

SuperNatural Aid

The adventure will require too much of the Hero for him to make it on his own accord. The stakes are too high, and the Hero will need to be fortified and reassured. Once the Hero becomes committed to the quest, a SuperNatural Aid will appear as a guide and protector along the journey, a figure who may not only help direct the Hero's path but also put the forces of nature and destiny at the Hero's side.

Crossing of the First Threshold

After committing to the call and gaining the assurances of the SuperNatural Aid, the Hero must then officially cross into the field of adventure. Very often he comes immediately upon the first Guardian barring his way forward. The Guardian stands between the Hero and an unknown realm full of danger and uncertainty. To deal with the Guardian of the First Threshold is risky business. This is no benevolent force as it stands at the outer limit of the Hero's current sphere of power and understanding. To continue his journey, the Hero must deal with the Guardian and sneak past him into the greater unknown.

Belly of the Whale

After crossing the First Threshold, the Hero must go through an initial sort of death and rebirth. The Belly of the Whale is a common mythological motif symbolizing the womb. The Hero doesn't immediately see his limitations removed and his sphere increased upon crossing the First Threshold. He must go through a sort of self-annihilation first. He must die, but not in the biological sense that he has come to the end of his life. He must be cleansed and leave his secular body behind. After appearing to die (i.e., entering the Belly of the Whale), the Hero emerges changed. The dying to his previous form of existence proves to be, in fact, an essential life-renewing act leading the Hero to a higher form of experience. Further, by dying to his old self, he moves closer toward his true self.

Road of Trials

As the Hero learns to take mastery over his new powers and the rules of this new world, he faces a perilous path of challenges. The ordeals he faces during this phase are a deepening of the problems he faced in crossing the First Threshold. The dangers have not subsided, and the questions about the Hero's character and future destiny remain unanswered. Many times these trials will come in sets of threes, and the Hero may at times stumble and even fail. There will also be momentary victories and glimpses of a world and existence as it is meant to be before the conflict continues.

Meeting with the Goddess

In this phase the Hero comes into contact with the embodiment of unconditional love. In this phase of all-powerful, all-encompassing love, the Hero finds assurance that at the conclusion of his soul's exile, the chaos and trials of the world will be set right and paradise will reign once again. This divine love, often signified in mythology by a female figure, is a unifying and life-bearing force connecting the Hero to eternity.

Temptation

Even as the Hero enjoys the reward of divine love, he may encounter temptation along the way to give up the eternal for the temporal. While this temptation is often experienced in mythology through the woman as the temptress, it could very well be any temptation that draws the Hero away from his quest. In this phase the Hero may become aware of his depravity—that everything he thinks or does is "tainted by the flesh" —and that even the woman, the symbol and source of life, may become an instrument of sin and death. He loses the assurances of reaching paradise, of his divine connection to the eternal, if he allows his newfound identity to be overrun by sin.

Atonement with the Father

In this phase the Hero must confront the thing that holds the ultimate power over his life, usually represented by the Father. This stage is also one of initiation, and as the Hero is properly prepared, he becomes like the Father (AT-ONE-MENT), but if he is initiated before he is ready, he won't be able to handle the powers that come with the Atonement. In many cases before the son can move in the direction of the Father, he must first learn to see the Father in the light of his mercy and grace. This is part of the growth process of the Hero as he comes to understand the inaccuracies of his infantile views of the Father as only a mercurial and vengeful force. As he endures the crisis and terror that are apt to come as part of the Atonement, he sees the truth about the Father. The world of crisis melts away into the life-breathing perpetual manifestation of the Father's presence.

Apotheosis

In this phase the Hero attains a divine state as he comes to understand that the Everlasting lives within him. The ego is finally set aside as the desires of his previous uninitiated state are left behind. He is free to enjoy the bounty of living in communion with the Father and as part of the Father. The Hero achieves peace and now is ready to receive the spiritual blessings of one who has faced the ordeals of setting his selfish desires and ambitions aside. Time and eternity are no longer disparate experiences but, rather, are connected. Death is not the end of life; it's the beginning of renewal.

The Ultimate Boon

All of the previous steps have prepared the Hero for the final step before beginning his return. In this step the Hero finally achieves the goal of his quest and gets his reward. He finds the magic elixir he has been seeking, and the image of indestructibility is finally realized. In some cases, if the Hero is ready, the boon allows the Hero to transcend the limits of his own understanding and personality. He gains perfect illumination: he is at one with the heavens. He convenes with a light and vision that go well beyond the limits of what he can describe or portray with human words or pictures. He has penetrated to the source of life itself and has received a gift that makes all of the trials faced on his journey worthwhile.

Refusal of the Return

Now that the Hero has completed his mission, it's time for him to bring his boon back to the world from where he came. This is not always easy for the Hero. Understandably, he may desire to remain in the presence of the bestower of the boon instead of returning to his common world to transfer that reward upon his fellow man.

Magic Flight

As the Hero attempts to return to his Ordinary World, he may encounter further resistance in his attempted departure. If the reward has been won against an opposition or a guardian of the boon, the Hero may find himself being pursued during his return. A chase of sorts may take place, and the hero may have to utilize any variety of evasive techniques to escape those forces that are hoping to bar his return to his world.

Rescue from Without

Eventually reality will come beckoning the hero back from his supernatural adventure. He may find himself guided back to the wakened state of his conscious world by the same force that ushered his way throughout the entire journey. That is to say, he may need supernatural assistance and encouragement as he deals with the dilemma of his return. Without a saving power's divine intervention, he may be tempted to remain or he may not even be aware that it's time to leave.

Crossing of the Return Threshold

Ready to return from that mystical place where the ego goes to die, the Hero faces one final ordeal. It is here that he is retested and fully cleansed so that he can be resurrected into ordinary life. As he crosses this final threshold, he must determine how to reintegrate himself into the world from which he came. He must determine how to knit the two worlds of his experience—the temporal and the eternal—together. He may find that his values have changed so much that the distinctions that once seemed important to him have lost their appeal. He may find it difficult to relate to those who can only see the world of their senses and not what lies beyond, as the Hero has seen.

Master of Two Worlds

Ultimately, the Hero will come to understand that the other dimension from which he is returning and the ordinary experiences of his life are actually not distinct from each other. What he has discovered in his journey is a fuller sense of reality—that the mystical dimension has always been there waiting to be integrated into his daily life. By losing his life, he has found it, and with that a wisdom has been born of humility about how to balance the material world with the spiritual world and the inner life with the outer life. With this mastery of both worlds, he is free to pour into his community the wisdom, love and insight that he has gleaned during the journey.

Free to Live

The Hero's mastery of both worlds also frees him from the fear of death, which in turn gives him the freedom to live. He is no longer anxious because his identity no longer finds its locus around his actions and deeds. Instead, he turns to the source of life itself, and on his knees he offers the fruit of those deeds as a living sacrifice. Time—the past and the future—is no longer keeping him in bondage, and so he lives fully present to all of creation in the knowledge that death will be defeated. His own ego has been subjugated, which gives him the greater capacity to love his fellow man and all the world.

Twenty-First Century Heroes

It may seem a stretch to consider our life in the twenty-first century in such mythic terms as just described. We might respond that "life doesn't really work this way." That's why we call them "myths." No, I don't expect a whale to swallow any of us, and I don't expect that we will go out and risk our mortal life tomorrow in search of an initiating experience. The Hero's Journey is not a prescription for taking unwarranted risks or quixotic adventures.

So what do myths generally and the Hero's journey specifically do for us in a technological world beside give us some of our favorite movies? Can they really help us make sense of a life informed by science and reason? Mythologist C. S. Lewis would respond that "Myth in general is not merely misunderstood history ... nor diabolical illusion ... nor priestly lying ... but at its best, a real unfocused gleam of divine truth on human imagination."[7] The right mythology may have a purpose even in a technological society. Our lives may grow richer if we become open to a more mythical perspective, not as an invalidation to reason, but as an extension of it. I'll explain what I mean by this in the next chapter.

CHAPTER III

THE HEAD AND THE HEART

ON A BRISK SEPTEMBER MORNING IN 1647, a carriage pulled up in front of a modest home in Paris inhabited by Étienne Pascal and his three children. René Descartes, the preeminent mathematician and philosopher in the world at that time, hopped out and knocked on the door. Descartes had returned to his home country of France on a short visit from self-imposed exile abroad. While on his visit, Descartes hoped to meet Étienne Pascal's son, a math prodigy named Blaise. The young Pascal's precocious talents intrigued Descartes. In particular, he had been struck by the genius of a mathematical paper that Blaise Pascal had written at the age of sixteen on the subject of conic sections.

The fifty-one-year-old Descartes spent the entire morning with Blaise. First, Blaise showed Descartes his latest invention, a mechanical calculating device that he had conceived of while helping his father with his job as a tax collector. The "Pascaline," as the machine became known, is considered by many to be the first computer in history.[1] The boy's genius stunned Descartes, and the conversation bounced around to other common interests. Blaise described experiments that he had been conducting to test his theories on the physics of a vacuum, and the two debated the best approach. After a few hours, Descartes took his leave to go to another appointment, but he returned the next day for a follow-up visit.

Three years before this meeting with Blaise Pascal, René Descartes had published *Principals of Philosophy*, one of the most important works of the seventeenth century, and had emerged as the most influential thinker in Europe. Some historians identify Descartes as the father of modern philosophy.[2] He is the one who coined the phrase, "I think, therefore I am." By the time Descartes visited with Pascal, a clear distinction had been drawn in intellectual and academic circles throughout Europe. The important question of the day, the dividing line between two world views, was whether one was a Cartesian, a follower of Descartes, or not.

By the morning of Pascal's meeting with Descartes in 1647, a revolution was underway in the world— not a political revolution, at least not initially, but a complete reframing of the foundational assumptions about knowledge, ideas and science. It was the dawn of the period historians call the "Enlightenment" or "Age of Reason." Both Descartes and Pascal's time on earth overlapped with that of Galileo Galilei, Thomas Kepler, Francis Bacon, and Isaac Newton, among others. Modern science was being born, and the discoveries of the age opened a new chapter for humankind, one that is still unfolding today.[3]

Saved by Reason?

For over a thousand years, all knowledge about both spiritual and scientific matters had found their authority with the Catholic Church. The belief in a fixed, harmonious and finite cosmos went all the way back to antiquity. Almost overnight the edifice of scientific belief in a fixed galaxy revolving around earth came crashing down, and with that many questions arose regarding nature, cosmology and religious authority. After centuries of faith in the infallibility of the church in all realms of life, nearly every assumption was suddenly called into question. Not since the emergence of Christianity itself had a civilization undergone a more radical upheaval to its very foundation than the one ushered in by the Age of Reason.[4]

It is impossible today to fathom how disorienting this tidal wave of science was to those living during that period. The people couldn't help but feel that they had lost their place in the world. They had imagined themselves the center of an enclosed harmonious and ordered universe. The discoveries of Copernicus, Galileo and Newton disintegrated peoples' notion of the cosmos and left the intellects of the time in a state of confusion. Into the void stepped René Descartes with a new solution, a new path to salvation for humanity. Descartes said, "I shall bring to light the true riches of our souls, opening up to each of us the means whereby we can find within ourselves, without any help from anyone else, all the knowledge we may need for the conduct of life." [5]

Descartes asserted that all knowledge for conducting life, a role traditionally ascribed to the church, should come from man's reason alone. The intellect was the only faculty man needed for life, and here the line in the sand was drawn. Was reason really sufficient to "bring to light the true riches of our souls?" Cartesians believed so.

Blaise Pascal would have his own answer to the question in due time, but after his meetings with Descartes, he continued for the next decade to make additional contributions in the fields of math, physics and medicine. Pascal tested the theories of Galileo and other mathematicians, culminating in his famous law of hydraulics, which states that pressure on the surface of a fluid is transmitted equally to every point in a fluid. He developed the theory of probability, which is still used today. Pascal wrote important papers on the theory of the vacuum and on the weight and density of air. He published a scientific paper on the calculation of an arithmetic triangle still known today as "Pascal's triangle." In addition to the first computer, he also invented the syringe, hydraulic lift, roulette wheel and wristwatch! And he accomplished all of this by the time he was in his early thirties.[6]

One night in November 1654, at the age of thirty-two, Pascal was preparing for bed when he experienced what could only be described as a spiritual conversion. Pascal received a vision that lasted for several hours late into the night. Pascal recorded the experience on a parchment sitting on his desk and called it the "Night of Fire." After Pascal's death, the parchment on which he had recorded the event was found sewn into the breast of his coat. He had carried it near his heart the rest of his life. His "Night of Fire" ended up becoming a pivotal moment in Pascal's life. From that point on, he shifted most of his energy and attention to religious and spiritual studies.[7]

In addition to Pascal's extraordinary scientific work, he would prove himself to be a prolific thinker in spiritual matters as well.

Today he might be better remembered for the inspiring body of Christian spiritual wisdom he wrote in the years following his "Night of Fire" than for his scientific accomplishments before it. Pascal's own views on knowledge challenged Descartes' notions about the divinity of rationalism. Pascal famously wrote, "The heart has its reasons which reason knows nothing of." While it might be tempting to read this to mean the heart is irrational and compulsive, that is not what Pascal meant. Pascal's own experience had demonstrated to him that reason alone, as Descartes had claimed, was not sufficient to understand life.

Pascal made the case that man has two faculties for comprehending truth: the head and the heart. The head is the seat of the rational intellect, which relies on scientific observation and logic to make sense of the world. The heart refers to intuition about things that are known to be true but that logic alone can't prove. The heart is the seat of creative imagination, desire and the will. The heart doesn't invalidate the intellect but allows a person to travel beyond it to a fuller understanding of the timeless questions about the meaning of life and the activities of God.

These two points of view have various nuances, which many other prominent thinkers have explored over the past four centuries. But there was a distinct shift of the pendulum beginning with Descartes and other thinkers during the Age of Reason. The Cartesians won out over the non-Cartesians such as Pascal. Authority on knowledge and truth shifted from the spiritual guidance of the church to the spiritual guidance of science and reason. In many ways a change was necessary, but history also suggests that the pendulum swung too far. The break with thousands of years of one worldview created an overreaction to another worldview "where all knowledge we need to conduct life" could be found through the intellect alone.

The implicit promise of the Age of Reason was that man could use science and technology to create a better world, to alleviate suffering and to form more just societies. However, the expected outcome wasn't what occurred. The Age of Reason birthed Imperialism, leading to the oppression and destruction of the cultures of non-Western nations for centuries. Wars didn't cease; technology just enabled man to annihilate himself with significantly greater efficiency and scale.

The Age of Reason led to the Industrial Revolution, which brought forth great progress in commerce but at the expense of basic human rights and the destruction of the environment.

By the middle of the twentieth century, many philosophers, writers and artists had also given up on rationalism. They looked at the world that had been promised by rationalism and modernity, and all they saw was suffering and inequality. One Great War was followed by another. Genocidal dictators continued to rise to power. Severe economic dislocations felt as destabilizing and as painful as ever. Postmodernism, with its abject pessimism, was born out of the disillusionment that resulted when reason didn't deliver all that it had promised. The Postmodern thinkers had lost both God and reason.

But technology and reason are not the problems. They have enabled wonderful advancements in many fields such as medicine, which have led to dramatic improvements in the quality and duration of life. Modern transportation has opened the globe for nearly anyone to explore. The Internet puts the entire body of the world's information at the fingertips of any person with a Wi-Fi connection. The benefits of reason and progress go on and on. The problem is that, while technology and reason may tell us how to organize and manage things, it's the heart that tells us why. Technology makes us far more efficient, but it doesn't dictate to what ends that efficiency is used.

So how does a person living in an advanced technological society with all of its demands and distractions reengage the heart? Can we have both God and reason?

Myth and Modernity

We concluded the previous chapter by discussing how a certain type of myth may help us live more richly today. However, myth lost its reputation during the Age of Reason and has never recovered. We may tolerate it as entertainment or as an artifact for studying ancient cultures, but it has fallen into disrepute as a means for understanding the world. Modern society sees myth through the lens of Descartes—as make-believe stories that prescientific civilizations came up with to explain what they couldn't understand without scientific inquiry.

Why did the sun rise every day in the East? Why were some harvests bountiful and others barren? Would the river flood again soon? We might ask why our modern scientific society needs stories to explain these things.

On the surface this may appear to be a positive development for humankind. Scientific reason freed man from the bondage of assigning supernatural explanations to natural events. And, although in one sense myths offered comfort in the face of uncertainty, in another sense myths sometimes proliferated wild and detrimental superstitions.

In our modern society, it's hard to understand how myth has much relevance to conducting life in a scientific world. In fact, we use the word *myth* today as a way of saying that some prevailing beliefs are lies. Consider a couple of headlines of articles I recently came across online: "12 Top Myths about Weight Loss" and "The 3 Myths of Listening." Our language has adapted around this term, and it's clear when we use the word *myth* today that we are implying that it's an old belief that has proven to be untrue by the discovery of new information.

In our modern predisposition to think of everything in terms of the head first, we have missed the point of myth altogether. We have ignored the potential impact that a mythical perspective of life can have on that other faculty that we have identified in this chapter—the heart. We have also misinterpreted the way pre-Age of Reason societies viewed myth. Our English word *myth* comes from the Greek word *methos*, which literally translated means "exemplary account."[8] *Methos* overlaps in meaning with the Greek word *logos,* from which we derive our English word *logic.* To the ancient Greeks, *methos* and *logos* were complementary in nature, whereas we think of them as being opposites. The Greek philosopher Aristotle, who spent most of his time meditating on the truth of *logos,* admitted that the lover of *methos* is also in a sense a lover of wisdom. Plato utilized myths extensively in his writings to drive home his broader philosophical points.

When the Greeks referred to the works of the poets as "myths," they weren't referring to the fact that the stories were fictional or false accounts. It was a complement referring to the fact that the poet was theorizing in hopes of persuading his audience. The philosophers would have likely agreed that the stories were fictional, but that wasn't the point. They were interested in discovering the *logos*—the universal truths governing existence and beyond. They recognized myths as being helpful to that understanding.

Ancient Greek historian George Grote wrote that myths depicted, "a past that was never present—a region neither approachable by the critic nor measurable by the choreographer."[9] In other words, myths are tales that go beyond common experience—even the ancients understood this. In this place beyond experience, the characters in the story exhibit mystical, heroic or divine power supreme to the natural world. A proper mythical story touches such a deep part of us that apart from the common storytelling elements, it can also be recognized by its effectiveness in instructing its audience in moral truth. It helps to bring unification to the chaos of the natural world and gives the community a sense of sacred purpose. It gives us a way of pursuing universal truths through story. "Myths are things that never happened but always are," wrote the Latin Philosopher Sallustius in the fourth century.

Author and mythologist Karen Armstrong says, "A myth is true because it is effective, not because it gives factual information." The intended recipient of the story doesn't have to believe in the historical or scientific verifiability of the story for it to be effective. What is more important is what the intended recipient takes from the story. This echoes Campbell's sentiment in *A Hero with a Thousand Faces* when he writes, "It has always been the prime function of mythology ... to supply the symbols that carry the human spirit forward, in counteraction to the other constant human fantasies that tend to tie it back."

Coordinating the Head and the Heart

Myth is a coordinator between the head and the heart. It begins in our mind through sensory experiences, but it offers to carry us beyond the mind. Let me tease this idea out with a metaphor: Picture a canyon with a deep crevice dividing one side from the other. One side of the canyon represents your intellect and sensory experience. The other side of the canyon represents your intuition, emotions and experiences that take you beyond your intellect and reason. A myth is not intended to sit on either side of the canyon. It's a bridge between the two sides and allows you to travel back and forth between them. A myth is a metaphor designed to provide the symbols that bring the intellect and senses to the edge of the canyon. From time to time, if the symbols are presented in the right order and context, you will find that you have traveled across the bridge and you will discover a whole different plane of meaning.

Campbell explains it this way: "Mythology is not a lie; mythology is poetry, it is metaphorical. It has been well said that mythology is the penultimate truth—penultimate because the ultimate cannot be put into words. It is beyond words, beyond images."[10] Myth allows for a more fundamental and innate understanding than our senses and intellect can grapple with.

C. S. Lewis understands myth in much the same way. He describes one of the great heroes from Norse Mythology (Balder) and suggests that the words of the story are just abstract symbols that move us toward an experience:

> *Myth does not essentially exist in words at all. We all agree that the story of Balder is a great myth, a thing of inexhaustible value. But whose version—whose words—are we thinking when we say this? For my own part, the answer is that I am not thinking of any one's words. No poet, as far as I know or can remember, has told this story supremely well. I am not thinking of any particular version of it. If the story is anywhere embodied in words, that is almost an accident. What really delights and nourishes me is a particular pattern of events, which would equally delight and nourish if it had reached me by some medium which involved no words at all.* [11]

Mythology is not the only medium that has this potential to draw us beyond the intellect into a different plane of experience. Art has always played this role, as has the natural beauty of the world around us. Isn't it true that the experience of beauty is one of those odd enchantments that defies explanation? Author David Skeel writes about beauty in his book, *True Paradox*: "The perception that beauty is real and that it reflects the universe as it's meant to be, but that it is impermanent and somehow corrupted, is the paradox of beauty."[12] It appeals to us through the senses and is real but also fleeting. It points us beyond itself to a transcendent truth.

When we encounter beauty, our intellect sends us scrambling for our cameras to try to capture a sublime moment, a sweeping vista or a stunning painting. But beauty won't allow us to bottle it up so easily. We try to analyze its effect on us afterwards, but words won't quite suffice. Beauty, like myth, draws us beyond the confines of our intellect. It strengthens our convictions because it reminds us of the potentialities of the life we are living and of the way things are meant to be but aren't quite yet.

Still, our rational side struggles to accept its limitations. Since Descartes deified "rationalism," we have four centuries of scientific progress to promote its omnipotence. Even many religious denominations have learned to shift their focus to appeal to the "rational" side of their followers. The weekly religious message emphasizes practical advice and action plans. The theology focuses on teasing out the factual and historical verifiability of its tradition, to build up in the followers all of the logical proofs they need to survive their encounters with skeptics. They work hard to satisfy the intellect. But something gets lost when we spend all of our time meditating over and proving formulas.

In a modern scientific world, it's much easier to control religious followers through their intellect than to point them toward a personal spiritual experience and revelation that a religious leader can't manage. The poetic aspect of religion gets reduced to prose when the best is a balance of the head and the heart. Karen Armstrong writes, "A theology should be like poetry, which takes us to the end of what words and thoughts can do."[13] This is also the role of music and rituals in religious services— to move the believer beyond the walls of the sanctuary. Of course, the head can't be ignored. We must satisfy it first, but only so we can complete our travels. Six-step plans, scriptural exegesis and rule-keeping requirements appease the head, but the real sustenance and transformation come through the heart. "The poet only asks to get his head into the heavens. It is the logician who seeks to get the heavens into his head. And it is his head that splits,"[14] wrote author G. K. Chesterton.

Getting Out of Our Heads

Where does this leave us with our journey into the mythical story we outlined in the previous chapter? My hope is that over these first few chapters, I can convince the intellect that this is a journey worth taking. I know from experience that the head would very much like to apply the brakes on the heart. The other side of the canyon can be a wild and mysterious place. Most of us have been trained to not trust the heart's intuition. Conventional wisdom suggests we should remain on the sidelines and wait for others to take the journey and then buy their book or listen to their podcasts. Today, we fill the head with information and hope it will suffice.

In Part II of this book, we will examine how the Hero's Journey can be applied to modern life, but no explanation can ever replace stepping into the mysterious journey personally. Life doesn't happen in a classroom, on the pages of a book or in a religious service. We will miss life's most profound experiences if we don't walk to the edge of the canyon and find the bridge that we can walk across into a fuller sense of the beauty and fundamental nature of life and creation.

Life doesn't happen in our intellect. It happens when we take a risk to go beyond the intellect. Consider the metaphor of learning to swim as an illustration of this limitation. Imagine for a minute you don't know how to swim and would like to become proficient enough so that you could comfortably swim across a pool without fearing for your life. How would you go about learning to do that? You could find a manual or video tutorials on swimming. They might teach you how to kick your feet properly or how to breathe. You could seek the advice of someone who teaches others how to swim, who might give you drills to practice or tips to use. You could interview someone who just learned how to swim about his or her own experience. If you dedicated yourself, you could become so advanced in your understanding of swimming that you might know more about the "science" of it than even Olympic swimmers.

The problem is that no amount of study can substitute for the actual experience of jumping into a pool and trying to make it back to the wall on your own. You can't learn to swim in your head. Only experience will teach you how the buoyancy (or lack thereof) of water feels or how the water resists you as you attempt to propel your body through it.

A description of swimming by a coach or in an instruction manual are abstractions of actual swimming. They are just words describing a mutual rational understanding of nature and how it works. It's not that the instruction isn't helpful. To the contrary, a swimming coach has spent much time studying and refining the techniques of learning to swim. The coach's practical teaching may accelerate the learning curve. However, even if you were convinced that you had the best swimming instruction in the world, if you had never swum before, you wouldn't jump off a boat in the middle of the ocean no matter how many years of training you had had on dry land.

As another example, would you learn what it's like to skydive without going up in a plane and jumping out? You could study the equations on gravity, watch videos of others' skydiving adventures and talk to skydiving experts, but they wouldn't substitute for strapping yourself to a parachute and feeling what it's like to have gravity suck you downward from 10,000 feet.

The head grasps for explanations for things that reason knows nothing of, but it's through the intuitions of the heart and its experience that the richness of life is discovered. What do you do when the beauty of nature or a song touches your emotions? One option is to just rest in the moment of that beauty. The other option is to try to understand why the beauty moves you so deeply. The moment you take the second option, you are no longer enjoying the beauty itself but, at best, enjoying the fact that you enjoyed something. Your head has transformed the real experience into an abstraction of it.

The richest human experiences elude logic in the sense that they can only be analyzed after the fact. Any time we try to analyze during the fact and move to the head, the experience is immediately over.

We have to then wait until the next time we are caught off guard and are free to just enjoy and experience truth in a different way. It is not that the head offers an inferior truth. It doesn't. But if we are always jumping to an explanation of an experience that is coming from the head, we miss some of the other truths that life offers.

A swimming teacher may help us learn to swim just as a pastor can teach us about God, but neither can replace what's intuited through the experience. If the head isn't enough to learn to swim, is it enough to answer the deepest metaphysical questions that haunt all of us at different times in our life, such as, "Why am I here on this earth?" "What is the point of all this?" "Who is God? " Myth offers a bridge into greater awareness of the potential answers to these questions.

But will any myth do for this purpose? It's not that we need to readopt old myths for our culture and society and start worshipping Zeus at the temple. That is not what I am advocating. What I am suggesting is getting to a point where we can open ourselves to experience stories and our own lives in mythical terms. As Campbell said, myth has always provided the symbols to carry the human spirit forward. But what symbols should we look toward today? Where can we find the sense of awe and wonder that will capture the imagination of our modern minds and bring us across the cavern between our heads and our hearts? Where can we find a story that can satisfy the modern intellect and its skepticism without destroying the mystical wonder of it all? As we embark on our own Hero's Journey, who can we look to for a guide? In the next chapter, I will lay out my case for a myth that can withstand both tests—that will have the approval of both the head and the heart while serving as a personal guide for our own real-life Hero's Journey.

CHAPTER IV

MYTH BECAME FACT

IT WAS SEPTEMBER 19, 1931, and three Oxford professors had just finished having dinner together on the campus of Oxford University's Magdalen College. The men continued their dinner conversation while they strolled along Addison Walk, a picturesque trail through a natural scenic area of the college. They headed past a low stone wall and turned through black wrought iron gates marking the entrance to the trail. They wandered along a dirt path bordered by a small creek with a lush green bank rising out of the water. Trees lined one side of the path, and on the other side, the silhouettes of the spires and towers of Oxford University rose against the darkening night sky.

One of the professors was a thirty-two-year-old tutor of English literature named C. S. Lewis whose friends knew him as "Jack." The other two professors joining Lewis that night included thirty-nine-year-old J.R.R. Tolkien, also a professor at Oxford, and thirty-five-year-old Hugo Dyson, a Shakespearean expert who taught at nearby Reading University. As the three men walked, their conversation turned to religion and faith, of which they had competing perspectives. As a teenager Lewis had become an ardent atheist, and his initial skepticism of religion only continued to grow in conviction as he became an adult. Tolkien, whom Lewis referred to as "Tolkiers," was a devout Catholic, and Dyson was a devoted Protestant. While the men did not share a common religious understanding, their love for literature, poetry and mythology engendered a certain mutual respect and admiration for each other. This was not the first time the conversation amongst these friends had found itself attending to spiritual matters, but the conversation on this evening had an uncommon character to it.

Lewis prodded Tolkien on what Lewis referred to as the "Christian myth." As a teenager Lewis had come under the influence of a private tutor, who introduced Lewis to a provocative book published by Sir James George Frazer called *"The Golden Bough."* Frazer, an anthropologist and mythologist, had spent years collecting and studying mythic stories from various cultures around the world. In the book Frazer concluded that religion evolved from myths and that both were human efforts to make sense of the frightening and incomprehensible. Frazer believed science was in the process of saving man from these peculiar superstitions.

Of particular controversy, Frazer had noted that in other myth traditions, there was a recurring story of a dying and resurrected god. In these myths the gods were usually associated with the cycle of nature, of agricultural societies in which plant life grew out of the ground, blossomed, died and returned to the soil before repeating the cycle. Frazer concluded that these other dying gods showed that the story of Jesus was a replica of other traditions and that theory became the foundation of what some have labeled the "anthropological argument" against Christianity.

Lewis loved the pagan myths, particularly Norse mythology. His mother had died when he was a young boy, and his father had checked out of his life at the same time, shipping Lewis and his brother off to various boarding schools. Lewis spent much of his childhood in the comfort of stories. In particular, he escaped to his own imagination by reading the great myths and even creating some of his own. In the best stories, Lewis experienced a profound emotion he called "Northernness," which was an indescribable sense of joy that left him with a feeling of intense longing.[1]

As the three professors walked, Tolkien observed that when Lewis met sacrifice in a pagan story, he didn't mind it at all. Lewis agreed that when he discovered the idea of a god sacrificing himself to himself, he was mysteriously moved. The dying and reviving gods such as Balder, Adonis and Bacchus all had a similar effect on Lewis.

Why, then, asked Tolkien, did Lewis resist the same internal movement when it came to Jesus?

Lewis realized that in the pagan stories, he was prepared to feel the myth as something profound and suggestive of meaning beyond his grasp, although he had no idea when and where these gods died because they weren't historical. Tolkien continued to press his point, convinced that the pagan myths were not the opposite of fact and that these stories were a way for the ancients to express deeper truths. Tolkien explained to the group that not only did the truth in myths come from God, but also that a writer of myths could do God's work in the world. Lewis would later note that at this point the "conversation was interrupted by a rush of wind which came so suddenly on the still, warm evening and sent so many leaves pattering down that the three men momentarily thought it was raining. They all held their breath, Tolkien and Dyson appreciating and enjoying the significance of the moment."

The discussion continued in Lewis's dormitory room on campus until the early morning hours. Lewis wouldn't wake up the next day as a Christian, but the wheels were in motion. In fact, they had been in motion for two years by the time Lewis had his fateful conversation with Tolkien and Dyson. He would recall that a couple of years previous to this evening, he had been startled by an offhand comment another one of his Oxford Colleagues, T. D. Weldon, an ardent atheist like Lewis, had made to him during a casual conversation.

Weldon had remarked, "Rum thing, that stuff of Frazer's about the Dying God, It almost looks as if it really happened once." Lewis was so jarred by the comment and that it had come from one of his atheist allies that he decided to read the Gospel accounts closely. What he found in them was something wholly different than other mythical stories. They were written in an "artless, historical fashion." Contrary to the pagan stories, Lewis noticed that the Gospels were painstakingly set in a particular time and place instead of the poetic otherworldliness characterized by pagan myths. Furthermore, there was no evidence that the story of Christ had anything to do with agriculture or fertility as the pagan stories had. Lewis wondered what the point was of a corngod if there was no promise of corn.

The first step for Lewis was to concede himself a theist. In his autobiography, *Surprised by Joy*, he recalls the night he accepted that perhaps he had been wrong about God's existence.

> *You must picture me alone in that room in Magdalen, night after night, feeling, whenever my mind lifted even for a second from my work, the steady, unrelenting approach of Him whom I so earnestly desired not to meet. That which I greatly feared had at last come upon me. In the Trinity Term of 1929 I gave in, and admitted that God was God, and knelt and prayed: perhaps, that night, the most dejected and reluctant convert in all England.[2]*

To be clear Lewis at this point was not a Christian, but his intellect could no longer keep him from rejecting the existence of a supreme being. He would grapple with his theology for several years, and it would be Tolkien and Dyson on that September evening in 1931 who would help open his eyes to the solution to his dilemma. Lewis outlined his problem this way: "The two hemispheres of my mind were in the sharpest contrast. On the one side a many-islanded sea of poetry and myth; on the other a glib and shallow 'rationalism.' Nearly all that I loved I believed to be imaginary; nearly all that I believed to be real I thought grim and meaningless."

Myth Became Fact

Lewis had not rejected Christianity because it claimed to be historical. He had rejected it because in trying to read it as a historical and factual account, he had failed to appreciate it mythologically. Therefore, he had not discovered the same joy and longing in the Jesus account that he had felt when reading the pagan accounts, which he read with his guard down. When he realized how he had missed this part of the story, it reconciled the "two hemispheres" of his mind. In Jesus, and only Jesus, did Lewis come to find that his head and heart could be fully reconciled. Later in life Lewis would write about the paradox of Jesus: "For this is the marriage of heaven and earth: Perfect Myth and Perfect Fact: claiming not only our love and our obedience, but also our wonder and delight, addressed to the savage, the child, and the poet in each one of us no less than to the moralist, the scholar, and the philosopher."[3]

For Lewis the power of Jesus's story is that it has all of the meaning and properties of a myth but with the critical distinction that it really happened. The miracle of Jesus Christ is that by becoming Fact, he does not cease to be a Myth. The Cross becomes the ultimate symbol for traveling between the intellect and one's creative imagination. For the first time, one could be both a philosopher and a poet. One could approach Jesus with the innocence of a child and the maturity of a traveled scholar. Within a couple weeks of his discussion with Tolkien and Dyson, Lewis would accept that Jesus Christ was who he said he was. Lewis would become one of the most significant Christian apologists of the twentieth century and a prolific writer of myths, most notably his children's series, *The Chronicles of Narnia.*

As for the objection that Frazer had raised about the similarity of Jesus to other pagan dying-god myths, Lewis and others found that this particular evidence was not a problem for Christians but, rather, was precisely what they should expect. Author G. K. Chesterton asked, "If the Christian God really made the human race, would not the human race tend to rumors and perversions of the Christian God? If the center of our life is a certain fact, would not people far from the center have a muddled version of that fact? If we are so made that a Son of God must deliver us, is it odd that Patagonians should dream of a Son of God?"

If the Hero's Journey is imagined repeatedly throughout history and still delights our sense of a coherent story today, is it possible that such stories all point toward a universal story—to one true story? It would be much harder to explain Jesus if every other Hero's Journey conceived was completely unique from his own. If God created man in his image with certain desires for the truth that Jesus reveals, it would be hard to conceive of the poetical side of man not dreaming up similar characters. If Jesus is what the heart longs for, it's probable that all kinds of stories from various cultures would reflect that longing, if only as dreams and premonitions. Lewis also wrote about this in detail:

To me, who first approached Christianity from a delighted interest in, and reverence for, the best pagan imagination, who loved Balder before Christ and Plato before St. Augustine, the anthropological argument against Christianity has never been formidable. On the contrary, I could not believe Christianity if I were forced to say that there were a thousand religions in the world of which 999 were pure nonsense and the thousandth (fortunately) true. My conversion, very largely, dependent on recognizing Christianity as the completion, the actualization, the entelechy, of something that had never been wholly absent from the mind of man. [4]

For Christians, God's grand truth for humanity is the death and resurrection of Jesus Christ. It shouldn't be surprising, then, that the rest of creation reflects and points toward this truth, including nature herself, the cycle of the seasons, the planting and harvesting of crops, the rising and setting of the sun. His truth is all around us. The similarities of our stories isn't an accident; it's a reflection of the one supreme story that reveals the creator to his created.

The Mingling of Philosophy and Mythology

We ended the previous chapter by suggesting that not just any myth would be capable of satisfying the scientific intellect and all of its skepticism without destroying the mystical wonder of the myth. Jesus's myth bridges this gap the way no other myth can. In Jesus we find that our intellect can be satisfied without diminishment at the wonder of his life and the Cross. The pagan myths C. S. Lewis loved were unrestrained by reason; they were purely imaginative. And even though some of these myths emerged from rational societies, the concept of merging the imaginative with the rational never occurred in any other tradition until Christianity. A mythologist such as Lewis understood this—that the myth was never intended to be scientific or historical—which is why the Jesus myth confounded him for so long. In the Jesus story, we get a radical departure because it presents itself not only as historical but also as philosophical.

G. K. Chesterton chronicles this interesting historical twist in his book, *Everlasting Man*: "The rivers of mythology and philosophy run parallel and do not mingle till they meet in the sea of Christendom. Simple secularists still talk as if the Church had introduced a sort of schism between reason and religion. The truth is that the Church was actually the first thing that ever tried to combine reason and religion."

To understand how Christianity is the first attempt to combine philosophy and poetry or reason and religion, it may be helpful to look at the opening lines of the Gospel of John:

"In the beginning was the Word, and the Word was with God, and the Word was God. He was with God in the beginning. Through him all things were made; without him nothing was made that has been made." (John 1:1-3 NIV)

"Word" as used in the passage comes from the Greek (the original language of the New Testament) word *logos*, which would have had an implication to the Gospel writer's Hellenistic audience, which we miss in translation today. By choosing the word *logos*, John is setting the stage for a shocking revelation. To a first-century audience, the word *logos* would have been recognized as a "philosophical" term. It had been first used by the Greek philosopher Heraclitus 600 years before the Gospel of John and was popularized by the fathers of philosophy: Socrates, Aristotle and Plato.

Logos referred to the philosophical notion that there was a harmonious, cosmic order to the universe, which could be discerned through human reason. Greek philosophers such as the Stoics would have understood the *logos* as a kind of divine but impersonal order governing the universe. When John says, "In the beginning was the Word and the Word was with God," he is evoking the Hellenistic concept of the perfect and grand organizing force undergirding the entire cosmos. For the Greek philosophers, the cosmos had nothing to do with the gods of myths. To the philosophers the highest form of knowledge came in the form of reason, and they pointed toward the order of the cosmos as proof that this was the case.

After introducing the "Word" in his prologue, the Gospel writer makes a connection that would have seemed insane to a Hellenistic audience reading John's Gospel. He writes, "The Word became flesh and made his dwelling among us." John is describing the Word as Jesus. It is difficult for us to understand how shocking this statement would have been to pagans at the time. John is saying that the logical and rational order of the universe is summed up in a single mortal life. He emphasizes his point by using the word *flesh* to describe the word *incarnate*. Stoic philosophy detested the material world (i.e., the flesh) as a vulgarization of the ideal. John is almost going to an extreme to point out that this *logos* made itself into lowly matter, of "flesh" (a piece of meat). To a Hellenistic audience, it would have been far less provocative for the Gospel to emphasize Jesus's divinity than his humanity. Stoic philosopher and second-century Roman emperor, Marcus Aurelius, would massacre scores of Christians on account of this one intolerable claim—that a single person was the focus of the entire cosmic order.

Before the Jesus myth emerged in the world, there was no real conflict between philosophy and mythology or between philosophy and religion because to the pagan world they encompassed two different spheres of thinking. The philosophers, including the Greeks, tried to explain the world through logical proofs. The mythmaker tried to explain the world through art. Neither side needed to concern itself with the other because they were concerned with two different issues. Philosophy operated in a world of prescription using reason to organize life. From the backdrop of the philosophical *logos*, Plato and Aristotle would develop theories for improving political organization, education, ethics, law, science and other fields. The mythmakers operated in a world of desire. Chesterton wrote, "We know the meaning of all the myths. We know the last secret revealed to the perfect initiate. And it is not the voice of a priest or a prophet saying 'These things are.' It is the voice of a dreamer and an idealist crying, 'Why cannot these things be?'" [6] The imagination of the mythologist centered on what it hoped to find: a world that should be but wasn't. Christians would say the Word (the *logos* of the philosophers) was also the answer to the yearning heart of the poet. The Christians had found the linchpin that could connect the two worldviews. Christians added one caveat: the Word could satisfy both the philosopher and the poet simultaneously if the Word was Jesus.

It's important to understand that from the beginning Christians pointed out that Jesus came as the fulfillment or the perfecter of *logos* and not as a replacement of the knowledge system developed by philosophers. It's clear that even first and second-century Christian writers held reason and revelation through Jesus to be complementary. Many of the pioneers of the faith revered the Greek philosophers. It's easy to discern the influence of the Greek philosophers on many of the giants of the Christian church, such as Justin Martyr (AD 100-165), Origen (AD 185-253), Saint Augustine (AD 354-430) and Thomas Aquinas (AD 1225-1274). In his Epistle to the Philippians, Paul also advocates a philosophical mindset: "Finally, brothers and sisters, whatever is true, whatever is noble, whatever is right, whatever is pure, whatever is lovely, whatever is admirable—if anything is excellent or praiseworthy—think about such things." (Phil. 4:8 NIV) In other words, philosophy and reason were foundational to Christianity.

What Christians recognized, though, is that reason had its limits and that the ultimate reality and ordering force of the universe was revealed in Jesus. In another one of Paul's epistles, he admonishes his recipients: "See to it that no one takes you captive through hollow and deceptive philosophy, which depends on human tradition and the elemental spiritual forces of this world rather than on Christ." (Col. 2:8 NIV) Paul isn't recommending that Jesus replace philosophical study. He says Jesus came to fulfill it, and believers should be leery of systems that find their authority and fulfillment elsewhere.

Even today skeptics like to think Christianity emerged as a rival to reason and that the church has been trying to suppress science and progress ever since. This is a gross misrepresentation of what happened and what Christianity espoused at its outset. By interpreting Jesus as the *logos* of the universe, Christians were actually saying that anyone who was pursuing knowledge through reason were, in a sense, pursuing Jesus. Some church fathers would even suggest that the pagan philosophers were a kind of proto-Christian and that they helped pave the way for Christianity. Pope Clement I (35-99 AD) wrote as the first pope, "For philosophy was a schoolmaster to bring 'the Hellenic mind to Christ.' Philosophy, therefore, was a preparation, paving the way for him who is perfected in Christ."[6] St. Augustine made an even more provocative claim: "For what is now called the Christian religion existed even among the ancients and was not lacking from the beginning of the human race until 'Christ came in the flesh.' From that time, true religion, which already existed, began to be called Christian."[8] The pagan philosopher's pursuit of knowledge wasn't misguided; it was just incomplete until the revelation of Jesus.

Subsequently, Christian theology emerged as a novel combination of philosophy and mythology held together by the historic action of one person. When the Gospel of John says Jesus is the Word, he is saying that all knowledge of both the head and heart come together in Jesus. If we want to unlock the mystery of life and of creation, the key is the story of Jesus as the fulfillment of both the intellect and the intuition of the heart.

Jesus the Hero

In the second chapter, I outlined the recurrent themes of the Hero's Journey, which can be found throughout the storytelling traditions of the entire world. It's easy to discern that Jesus traveled the Hero's Journey, too. The Gospel accounts clearly articulate the same themes. Jesus shows up at the Jordan River, an ordinary carpenter from an ordinary town named Nazareth. He emerges from the river, crosses into the wilderness and initiates the adventure that will change the world forever. He experiences all of the limitations of his humanity and all of the misgivings of his quest. Temptations, trials, betrayal and Threshold Guardians seek to thwart his destiny. The Spirit serves as his SuperNatural aid throughout the journey. His death is both literal and figurative, bringing final Atonement with the Father. He is resurrected into the world to bestow the gift of his journey to the community of humanity, having defeated death and sin so that those who follow him might have eternal life. The New Testament begins with the quintessential Hero's Journey, and all other great Hero's Journey stories point toward it.

When I first read about Joseph Campbell's description of the Hero's Journey, I thought it offered a profound road map for living. But when I contextualized Campbell's observations about stories with the promise of Jesus's life, I realized that the Hero's Journey was more than just an instruction manual. The myths were not just symbolic expressions to help us understand existence or what happens after death. The myths were not just lessons on the art of living; they were, in fact, pointing toward the ultimate expression of life. God broke into the history of the world and into the plane of human consciousness to give us more than a model for imitation. Jesus is no long-lost character from an unmarked time and place. He is of history at the same time that he is beyond it. And he offers to become a living, active participant in our own hero's quest—even today.

Without Jesus's interruption we would be left to the limitations of our own imaginative powers, always yearning, as Lewis did, for those fleeting moments of clairvoyant joy. Jesus makes it possible for the poet lamenting, "Why can these things not be" to finally experience the peace that they will be. All the other Heroes we love in stories are a reminder of an eternal desire. We humans were made for stories because our most accurate understanding of the *logos* of creation comes through one perfect story. We have been telling it over and over again without even knowing why. The story moves and delights us and never grows old. If we will be image-bearers of one true God, his story should reveal most accurately what he is like and so should ours. And that is what we find with Jesus. Even Joseph Campbell, who disavowed his own Catholic heritage, wrote, "The sign of the cross has to be looked upon as a sign of an eternal affirmation of all that ever was or shall ever be. It symbolizes not only the one historic moment on Calvary but the mystery through all time and space of God's presence and participation in the agony of all living things."[9]

The belief that Jesus is both myth and fact results in a mystical transformation of the believer. "Therefore if anyone is in Christ, they are a new creation: old things are passed away; behold, all things are made new." (2 Cor. 5:17 NIV) Every Hero's Journey requires that the Hero die to some old way of living in order to be reborn into a more fully alive condition. Until we take this quest, we are just shadows of who we were intended to be. Jesus's life means our quest will not be in vain. He came as the fulfillment of God's promise: "I will give you a new heart and put a new spirit within you; and I will remove the heart of stone from your flesh and give you a heart of flesh." (Ezek. 36:26 NIV)

Those of us who would venture into this story alongside Jesus are no longer slaves to our fallen nature. We experience a new identity, one in which the fear of death is replaced by the affirmation that the eternal order for which we desire is already upon us, dwelling in our new hearts of flesh.

The other great promise that follows from this transformation is that those of us who would know the Hero of all Heroes will not just bear witness to the glory of his quest but will share in it. At the end of the Gospel of Matthew, Jesus prays, "Father, just as you are in me and I am in you. May they also be in us so that the world may believe that you have sent me. I have given them the glory that you gave me, that they may be one as we are one—I in them and you in me—so that they may be brought to complete unity." (John 17:21-22 NIV)

God's primary means for initiating his loving power in the universe today comes through his Heroes who are being remade in the image of the *logos*. "For the eyes of the LORD range throughout the earth to strengthen those whose hearts are fully committed to him." (Chron. 16:9 NIV) God is searching for the Heroes through whom he can continue to share his power through the stories they are writing with their lives.

The context of our lives can best be interpreted through Jesus's life and his perfect Hero's quest. Paul writes, "I have been crucified with Christ; and it is no longer I who live, but it is Christ who lives in me. (Gal. 2:19 NIV) If this is true that Jesus dwells within us, we can see how our story will reflect his. It means that while our lives are certainly factual they may also be mythical.

Jesus can walk with us because he is God, but he was also fully human and understands the limitations of our humanity because he dealt with them, too. He grew weary and thirsty. He faced temptation. He felt loneliness and doubt in his final hours, and he experienced the agony of the crucifixion. Yet he completed his quest so that we could complete ours through his indwelling presence in our hearts. Our quest is not just symbolic or psychological. It's real. We are meant to be his apprentices, learning from him as we take our place in the creative activity of the *logos*.

Jesus has only one question for us before we begin our journey: "Will you follow me?" The road ahead is neither safe nor ordinary. Our life can have some of the substance of the immortal legends dreamed up by the great mythmakers. We just need eyes to see it as such and the heart to experience Jesus as more than history but as the mythological guide affirming our greatest joy and deepest desire.

CHAPTER V

FAITH IN THE MYTH

FAITH, WRITES THE AUTHOR OF THE LETTER to the Hebrews, "is confidence in what we hope for and assurance about what we do not see." (Heb. 11:1 NIV) In Faith a believer submits to the notion that there may be truth beyond the grasp of the intellect. In the previous chapter, I asserted that Jesus claimed a unique place in the history of myth. His life might have the same effect of the great myths drawing us toward a world of mystery and wonder but at the same time complementing a rational-scientific worldview. What we do with this notion about Jesus is a question of faith. Is Jesus just a myth? Is he just a historical person? Or is he somehow both? Is it reasonable to have "confidence" in what Jesus says he offers and "assurance" about who he says he was? Faith is what we do when we reach the end of what can be validated scientifically.

Those who believe that truth can be discovered beyond the intellect face a daunting challenge today. Philosopher Dallas Willard explained the environment confronting a spiritual point of view this way:

> We live in a culture that has, for centuries now, cultivated the idea that the skeptical person is always smarter than one who believes. You can be almost as stupid as a cabbage, as long as you doubt. The fashion of the age has identified mental sharpness with a pose, not with genuine intellectual method and character. Only a very hardy individualist or social rebel —or one desperate for another life—therefore stands any chance of discovering the substantiality of the spiritual life today. Today it is the skeptics

who are the social conformists, though because of powerful intellectual propaganda they continue to enjoy thinking of themselves as wildly individualistic and unbearably bright. [1]

The skeptic shudders at the word *faith* because what it really entails has often been misinterpreted. Also, I suspect that many people who say they "believe" in certain spiritual truths feel awkward about how to reconcile their faith with reality and hope they can ignore the tension they feel between the two. The good news is that faith and reason can be reconciled or, rather, have been reconciled. Jesus the fact and Jesus the myth point toward a truth that doesn't stand in the way of reason but perfects it. For the duration of this chapter, I hope to show that faith in Jesus may awaken us to the mystery of our existence while complementing the way we conduct our lives in a scientific world.

Pascal wrote, "Faith indeed tells what the senses do not tell, but not the contrary of what they see." Faith is neutral to reason in that there is no natural evidence for or against it. We could debate the purpose of human existence (eschatology), and one point of view might claim cosmic accident. Another point of view might say humans exist to glorify God and enjoy him forever. Neither one of those claims is irrational in the sense that it hypothesizes a view that can be disproven through scientific observation. In that sense God's activity cannot be proven, and neither can his absence. We may assume there is an objective truth that exists, but it would be irrational and contrary to science to suggest that we can know in a scientific way the entire truth of creation. Reason demonstrates that some truth is beyond reason. The rational intellect recognizes its limitations but through faith becomes open to the possibility that the heart can still be illuminated with some greater insight.

Faith devoid of reason is a problem for the skeptic for good reason, but it's also a problem for the believer. Comparative religious scholar Karen Armstrong observes, "We have domesticated God's transcendence. We often learn about God at about the same time as we are learning about Santa Claus; but our ideas about Santa Claus change, mature and become more nuanced, whereas our ideas of God can remain at a rather infantile level."[2] When we take the naive approach and avoid asking difficult questions in order to have faith, we will eventually come to a crisis in our life, and an immature and untested Faith will have a hard time dealing with it.

Trappist monk and author, Thomas Merton, wrote that when faith begins as an intellectual assent recognizing its own limitations, then "it perfects the mind, it does not destroy it. It puts the intellect in possession of truth which reason cannot grasp by itself.[3]" Reason gives us the best theology, but it's the heart that interprets it. The head conceives of an explanation of the Trinity but an attempt to approach that reality requires the heart.

The Truth of the Resurrection

If faith does not require the suppression of the intellect, we might ask, "Then what about Jesus?" Skeptics may raise many fair and rational objections to Christianity and religion in general—such philosophical questions as "Why does suffering exist if God is good?" or scientific objections about the age of earth and evolution that appear out of step with the Bible. My intent is not to write an entire apologetic covering the various hang-ups a secular person might have with faith. Instead, I want to highlight one particular piece of evidence, which provides the hinge for all the rest of the discussions and questions surrounding faith in Jesus.

The starting point for the reasonableness of faith in "Christianity" is Jesus's resurrection, the answer to the question, "Is Jesus myth and fact at the same time?" Without the resurrection Christianity is a tree without roots, easily toppled over. With the resurrection all other questions surrounding the mysteries or problems of faith can be answered in due course. What we believe about the resurrection is the pivotal question, the one that must inform all other questions related to the Christian faith. Why is this question so vital to the discussion of faith? Because if it were true that a man entered history, predicted his own death and resurrection, and then succeeded in pulling it off, we would probably want to take as true the other things he said as well. What other evidence would we need?

Any "Christian" faith begins and ends with the Hero, Jesus, and what we believe about the nature of his death and the days that followed it. We cannot say he was just a wise and great teacher, because that ignores the rest of his claims that he came to forgive sins, replace the moral law and offer the way to God. He was either a charlatan, a madman or who he claimed to be.

Of course, the modern mind has reasons to be skeptical about Jesus's resurrection, as that is not an achievement our science can easily account for. My objective is to show that, while belief in the paradox of Jesus can't be proven, it is not an irrational conclusion either. The intellect will allow us to see that the affirmation of the paradox of Jesus is no more, and perhaps less presumptuous than the position that denies his resurrection. The burden of proof is not all on the believer. The skeptic has to explain some fairly astounding evidence, too. What we choose to believe after the intellectual arguments I will set forth is a question only faith can answer.

What the First Believers Believed

There seems to be little question that Jesus was a historical person. Author and biblical scholar, Bart D. Ehrman, writes that Jesus "certainly existed, as virtually every competent scholar of antiquity, Christian or non-Christian, agrees and that the existence of Jesus and his crucifixion by the Romans is attested to by a wide range of scholars, including Josephus and Tacitus. While scholars differ on the historicity of specific episodes described in the Biblical accounts of Jesus, the baptism and the crucifixion are two events in the life of Jesus that are subject to 'almost universal assent.'"[3] The question up for debate is not whether Jesus existed in history (there seems reasonable enough evidence to assume he did), but whether he showed himself to his followers three days after his crucifixion.

What exactly did the people who knew Jesus believe after his death? This is an important question because the Christian faith is built on their interpretation of the events surrounding it. A clear answer to this question can be found in the following creed Paul included in his letter to the Corinthians:

For what I received I passed on to you as of first importance: that Christ died for our sins according to the Scriptures, that he was buried, that he was raised on the third day according to the Scriptures, and that he appeared to Cephas, and then to the Twelve. After that, he appeared to more than five hundred of the brothers and sisters at the same time, most of whom are still living, though some have fallen asleep. Then he appeared to James, then to all the apostles, and last of all he appeared to me also, as to one abnormally born. (1 Cor. 15:3-8 NIV)

It may not be an easy creed for the skeptic to accept, but it isn't complicated. What the author, Paul, is communicating in this passage is not intended to be mythological at all. This creed wasn't created generations after Jesus's death. This creed was given to Paul by those who knew Jesus personally.

One of the points some scholars have made in their questioning of Christianity is that the Gospels were written some forty or more years after Jesus's death. The first Gospel written was Mark's and is believed to have been completed around AD 70 (Jesus died in AD 30). Critics have sometimes used this to speculate on the motives and authenticity of the Gospel accounts. These critics reason that the authors were writing about a generation after Jesus, and therefore the miracles they wrote about may have been added later. Some hypothesize that the story developed in the same way as other oral legends, that is, new details were added as the story was passed down and the story evolved; classic myth elements are added, even though the story started as historical or biographical. While this is a shallow argument for many reasons beyond the scope of what we intend to cover here (i.e., the Gospel was written down when people who were witnesses to the event were still alive, not generations later), the creed Paul shared doesn't come from the Gospel accounts. It's a creed that was developed by the people who knew Jesus and gave testimony to his resurrection.

Historians do not dispute that a man named Paul lived and traveled around the Mediterranean and wrote letters to the churches he helped establish. These letters make up the bulk of the New Testament after the four Gospel accounts. Because of these letters, we know Paul visited Jerusalem not long after Jesus's death and resurrection, and he met Jesus's brother, James. The creed given above that Paul conveyed to the church in Corinth came directly from the people in Jerusalem—the eyewitnesses to the claims made in their creed. They developed the creed, one would assume, for the same reason any creed is developed, which is to establish the core beliefs of the group in a way that can be memorized and translated to others without confusing the details. [4]

This creed gives a clear picture of what it originally meant to be a follower of Jesus. The claims about Jesus's death and resurrection weren't added by hearsay or later authors with an agenda. This is what the people who knew Jesus and were his followers believed about him. They were on the ground in Jerusalem on that fateful day. They were there for the first persecution of Christians in Jerusalem a year or so before Paul's visit. It's one thing to believe in a messiah (as there were others in those days who claimed to be) while that person is alive. It's another thing entirely to believe in that person while that person is still alive, to watch that person die in the most horrific, humiliating and unexpected way imaginable and then still believe that that person is the Messiah. The crucifixion would seem to be all the evidence his followers needed to conclude that they were wrong that this person might be a prophet, but he was certainly not the Messiah. Some other information had to be available to them, information that was so undeniable that these early followers would risk everything in continuing to claim the man who died with the criminals on Cavalry was the savior. To conclude, as some have tried, that the central belief of the nascent Christian movement was something other than the confirmation of a physical resurrection isn't supported by the evidence.

Effect on Eyewitnesses

To understand how unexpected the impact of this event would have been on the witnesses to Jesus's resurrection, it's important to understand what they were expecting and the inexplicable disappointment they would have felt upon his death. The first eyewitnesses were all Jews, and for over 400 years, the Jews had been waiting without a word from God for the Messiah to come. Their hopes and dreams centered on the reestablishment of the Jewish state under a new king who would lead a revolution against their oppressors (i.e., the Roman Empire) and overthrow their rule. This is what the people Jesus ministered to were expecting from the Messiah. If the Messiah came, he would be expected to come as a revolutionary leader who would relaunch the Jewish kingdom.

The Messiah was not someone who they thought of as a divine being. They certainly had no concept of the Trinity theology adopted by Christians. The Messiah they were expecting would be a man much like King David, and like David, God would favor him and grant him a blessing to do mighty works. The proof they expected was not the defiance of death but a leader who would deliver the kingdom of the Jews from exile. They didn't expect a God walking around with them but, rather, a man who God would ordain to accomplish great things in the Jewish homeland.

Jesus's claim of being the Messiah, while provocative, was not nearly as provocative as his symbolic actions and claims to be the replacement of the Jewish law and its temple—claims he made repeatedly. The law and the temple were the central symbols of the Jewish faith. For Jews the temple was where God manifested himself in the world and where the law was given directly by God to allow Israel to mark itself in order to receive his divine favor. First-century Jews believed that the primary reason for their nation's state of subjugation to a pagan authority was because of the sins of the nation. [1]

The emergence of the Messiah would have had to mean that their sins were forgiven by God. The Messiah was supposed to invigorate the temple and the law, not predict their eminent decline, as Jesus did. For the Jewish high leaders who condemned Jesus's point of view, the greater blasphemy was not that Jesus claimed to be the Messiah, but that he claimed he could grant forgiveness and would set up a new temple and a new law for the Jewish people. This was not a claim of a Messiah; this was a claim that only God could make.

These expectations made those who continued to profess their belief in Jesus such a profound testament to the idea that the resurrection was real. Those who were eyewitnesses to the life of Jesus and continued to live by the creed cited earlier were not rewarded for their faith during their lifetime. Many of them were imprisoned, tortured and killed. The term "Christian" was first used as a derogatory term. These were not people who were tolerated by their community of other Jews or pagan religions. Jesus's disciple Thomas was stoned to death for his continued devotion to Jesus after Jesus's death. Peter was crucified upside down for his adherence to the belief that this man he had known in flesh and blood, the man he witnessed incomprehensibly detained by the Roman authorities, the man he had seen nailed to a cross was, in fact, the savior whom he and the people had been waiting for.

Try to imagine Peter and the other followers' dejection on the day of Jesus's death. What should they make of all the things Jesus had taught, and what should they make of the miracles they saw? What could they possibly believe now? The game was over. What could have assured Peter to walk so fearlessly that he would go to his own crucifixion for his belief in a risen Messiah? He had nothing to gain from that belief here on this earth. What could have convinced him to continue other than his belief in a risen Jesus? It's hard to believe the apostles willfully lied about what they saw. People lie because it benefits them, but there were no benefits to perpetuating their story unless the story was true.

Furthermore, the people who knew Jesus didn't scatter for long the way they did with other false messiahs. How can we explain the life of the people who knew Jesus if they weren't convinced that he had risen from the dead? How could this small sect of believers start a revolution that would reach the entire world and change the fabric of the most powerful empire in the world? If he had died and had not been resurrected, it would have violated every expectation that they had ever had about the Messiah. It would not have made sense to proclaim what they did. Perhaps some of them could have taught the lessons he taught them. But their creed wasn't a summary of Jesus's Sermon on the Mount or other teachings. It wasn't a retelling of his various miracles. What the people who knew Jesus codified in their creed didn't leave any doubt about what they believed to be the most important about Jesus.

Yes, Jesus's teachings may be authoritative and insightful. Yes, he may have made miracles a regular occurrence to his followers. These shouldn't be discounted, but the starting point of Christianity is the miracle of Jesus's journey as he overcomes death and is resurrected. Jesus's death should have ended the movement he began, but his death was only the beginning, and that is very difficult to reconcile if something more than death had not been witnessed by those who knew Jesus.

Historical Impact

The impact of this small group of Jesus's followers is unprecedented in history. There are 2.3 billion people in the world today who identify themselves as Christians, and 178,000 new converts join the movement every day.[6] Over 100 million new Bibles are sold or given away every year in 2,426 different languages.[7] The movement that began after the death of a single man in the Palestine region of the Roman Empire continues today in communities of Christians in every country in the world.

With the scope and scale of Christianity, it is easy to forget from what humble beginnings it was born. Given the opposition toward Christianity and its scarce resources, it's a historical miracle that it even survived its first 100 years. How could a few hundred Jews far from any political or economic centers of influence initiate a revolution that would fundamentally alter the society and culture of the mightiest empire the world has ever known? These normal folks—fisherman, tax collectors, farmers and house servants—believed so fiercely in the truth of a resurrected man that the history of the world pivoted around them.

They faced persecution first from their Jewish brethren who saw this perpetuation of the belief in the risen Messiah as heresy. They were cut off from their Jewish heritage, and not only were they cast out from the culture and society of their ancestors, but they also were imprisoned, threatened and sometimes murdered because of it. A man named Saul held a particular disdain for the Christians and watched as they were murdered. In repeated testimony, he described a miracle that altered his destiny and the church's. The miracle convinced him to change his name to Paul and become the leader of bringing Jesus's teachings to the gentiles.

Within a generation of Jesus's death, the Christians had also drawn the ire of the Roman Empire itself. In AD 64 Nero blamed a fire in Rome on Christians and began the first systematic persecution in which "multitudes" of them were tortured and killed for their beliefs. This persecution proceeded off and on throughout the Roman Empire for the next 200 years. Christian worship was not only illegal, but also intensely dangerous for much of the first 200 years of Christianity's existence. But amazingly, with each Christian martyr, the movement didn't lose followers; rather, it gained even more momentum and more followers. In AD 380 the emperor, Constantine, decreed that Christianity would be the new official religion of the Roman Empire.

Whether or not one believes in a risen Jesus, there is no denying that he is the most influential person in the history of the world, and there is no one else who comes even close. But it's also shocking that this is the case, given the circumstances facing the first generations of those Christians who followed Jesus and who were closest to the resurrection. On paper it should not have succeeded; Jesus's followers were the ultimate underdogs for establishing a new religion that would fundamentally shape society for the next 2,000 or more years. Furthermore, nearly every other segment of their society stood in opposition to their beliefs and worldview. Could what followed be explained if Jesus had been just an ordinary carpenter who told great parables?

Not the Story That Should Have Been Told

If you were trying to invent a new religion in Palestine 2,000 years ago, the Gospel accounts would not have been your chosen marketing strategy. What is startling about them is their level of honesty about some details that would have been convenient for the Gospel writers to ignore or downplay. When you consider their historical and cultural context, it's difficult to conceive why some details were relayed the way they were unless they were true; some details are just too problematic to be fabrications.

For example, all the Gospels tell us that women discovered Jesus's empty tomb and were also some of the first eye-witnesses to his resurrection. This is a problem for a first-century audience because of women's inferior status in that society. Women had such scarce credibility that their testimony was not admissible in court. The Gospel writers would have likely felt a lot of pressure to take more creative license with this fact in the story. A woman's testimony was believed to be unreliable, so the best explanation for its inclusion would be that the Gospel writers were trying to relay the true details of the story. If they were making this story up, they wouldn't have had women discovering the empty tomb.

After Jesus is crucified, the leadership of the church falls to the disciples who followed Jesus around during his life. But the Gospels continually point out the disciples' ignorance and faithlessness. On multiple occasions we read of Jesus's disappointment and dismay at the men who would ultimately bear his message. Why would the Gospel writers portray the fathers of the church in this way if they were trying to fabricate a good marketing strategy for the movement? They portray Peter, the "rock" on which the church is built, as impulsive, prideful and hardheaded. He also makes the grave mistake of denying Jesus—not once, but three times. Why would someone fabricate these accounts if they weren't true?

There were other messianic movements of the era, but none ever claimed a resurrected messiah except this one. These were not irrational people. A resurrection would have been as shocking to them as it is to us today. The only options for other messianic movements were to scatter or proclaim a new leader. As we have discussed, a crucified messiah wasn't even a category, and a resurrected body didn't make sense on multiple levels. It didn't make sense because bodies didn't resurrect any more often in the ancient world than they do today. Secondly, the prevailing Greek thought of the day was that the spirit was good and that the physical world and the body were corrupt. Why would a soul, having escaped the defilement of the body, return to it? That didn't make sense either. The crucifixion would have been an embarrassment to any other messianic movement. Furthermore, the resurrection wouldn't have seemed possible physically or desirable philosophically. Yet, this is what became celebrated and codified as the defining point of the Jesus movement. This doesn't seem like an outcome that a group of fisherman would have invented on their own.

Then there is the tomb itself. The tomb had to be empty because, if someone had claimed to have seen a risen person, the multitude of people hoping to squash the movement could have just gone to the tomb and produced the body, and the story would have been over. But that never happened. New Testament Biblical Scholar, N. T. Wright summarizes the shocking historical context of the resurrection this way: "The early Christians did not invent the empty tomb and the meetings or sightings of the risen Jesus.... Nobody was expecting this kind of thing; no kind of conversion experience would have invented it, no matter how guilty (or how forgiven) they felt, no matter how many hours they pored over the scriptures. To suggest otherwise is to stop doing history and enter into a fantasy world of our own."[8]

The First Universal Myth

Since we have been discussing Jesus as both myth and fact, I want to point out one interesting mythological break that makes the Jesus story even more convincing in that context. His story is the first time in history that we find a mythical God making a jump from the tribal to the universal. Christianity emerged from the tradition of the Hebrews, and the biblical Old Testament is full of language that echoes a tribal ethnocentric view of God. "You will be my people and I shall be your God," speaks God in the book of Jeremiah. (Jer. 30:22 NIV) Throughout mythology gods had always been considered in relationship to the tribe and its unique needs. The God of the Jewish Bible is often described as the God specifically of the Hebrews as opposed to the gods of the other ethnic groups that lived among them.

On the other hand, the Jewish tradition does have a peculiarity compared to all the other mythologies of the world. The Jews stood out against all of the other traditions of the region and virtually every other mythology found throughout history because of their belief in only one God. Greco-Roman culture was particularly undiscerning about adding new members to their pantheon of gods. While visiting Athens, Paul noted that the Athenians even have an altar constructed "TO AN UNKNOWN GOD" just in case they missed one.

In a break from tribal tradition, the Jews predict that God is not going to just be for their group forever. A revolutionary concept emerges in the poetry and prophetic writings of the Jewish tribe. They begin to presume that God is not exclusive to their group. According to the prophet Isaiah God said, "And I, because of what they have planned and done, am about to come and gather the people of all nations and languages, and they will come and see my glory." (Isa. 66:18 NIV)

Jesus once again stands out from the other mythic heroes. He comes as the fulfillment of a novel monotheistic culture's belief that God would one day reconcile the world to himself through a savior. And while the savior would emerge from the heritage of the Jews, he would come for all of mankind. This great monotheistic culture had survived for thousands of years by delineating clearly its ancestral and religious heritage (Was there ever a more permanent mark of who qualified for inclusion than the mark of circumcision?), and, as predicted, Jesus invites everyone into it.

If there is a God of the universe, would we not expect him to come forth as a universal God, approachable by anyone who has faith in him? Christianity enters the scene and makes a historical leap from gods of tribes to one God of the whole universe, a God who will come forth and instruct his disciples to "Go into all the world and preach the gospel to all creation." Paul describes this transition when he points out that becoming God's people is no longer about physical circumcision (the mark of the Jew) but about circumcision of the heart (acceptance of a resurrected Christ). Again, this is not the outcome we would expect; the indelible culture and tradition of the Jews endures against all odds for thousands of years as though its identity as a group is inspired by God. And it makes this novel leap from a tribal myth to a myth that the entire world can inherit. If one believes in an omnipotent force in the universe, I believe it makes sense for that omnipotent force to have something to say about all of mankind and not just one tribe. And that is precisely what emerged in a world that didn't have notions of monotheism or universal gods.

The Question of Faith

As we ask ourselves what we can reasonably believe, we can make the following assumptions regarding Jesus: he was a real person, he was crucified, his tomb was empty, hundreds of people claimed to have seen him resurrected, and, based on those claims, the most unexpected and significant movement in the history of the world began. This is not wishful thinking; these are the most logical assumptions we can bring to the question of Jesus's resurrection. But what conclusions can we draw from these assumptions? That is a question faith must answer.

I recognize that there are other questions and reasons people reject or walk away from Christianity. Most of them have nothing to do with Jesus but more often the way his so-called followers have represented (or misrepresented) him. My intent is not to solve all those issues but to point back to the central question of the Christian faith, the one that holds the key to all the other objections that may arise - the question of Jesus's resurrection. And while we cannot understand the truth of the resurrection through our intellect alone, submitting to it doesn't require a forced suppression of the intellect either. Pretending that doubt doesn't exist isn't the path to faith. Jesus offers a bridge between the life we experience in our minds and the deeper truths revealed in our hearts. This final step of traveling across the bridge cannot be done for us. Nor can the reality of the experience be "proven" to others.

As we walk the Hero's Journey in our own life, Jesus can serve as just another example to emulate—no different than Balder, Osiris or Dionysus. Or through the power of his own life, he can transform us into something new altogether and connect our small stories to the grand story of the universe. The question Jesus asks each of us is the same question that he asked his disciple Peter: "But who do you say I am?" (Mat. 16:15 NIV)

CHAPTER VI

SETTING THE STAGE

"INJUSTICE ANYWHERE IS A THREAT TO JUSTICE EVERYWHERE." You may have heard these words before. Dr. Martin Luther King Jr. penned them from a jail cell in Birmingham, Alabama, in the spring of 1963. This is one of many quotable lines from King's open letter addressing white Christian clergy in the South during the civil rights movement. In the letter King admonished the church, and its leaders to play the role the church was designed to play from the beginning—to be a movement that disrupts the status quo. Many southern white clergy recognized the injustice of segregation, but some thought King and his movement should take a more conciliatory approach to its resolution. While sympathetic to the civil rights movement, some didn't approve of King's tactics. Instead of the protests King organized to "agitate" the community, a group of white clergy wrote King an open letter in a newspaper suggesting that he focus on negotiation and allowing the justice system to run its course.

In his response to these calls for negotiation, King writes, "I have traveled the length and breadth of Alabama, Mississippi and all the other southern states. On sweltering summer days and crisp autumn mornings I have looked at the South's beautiful churches with their lofty spires pointing heavenward. I have beheld the impressive outlines of her massive religious education buildings. Over and over I have found myself asking: What kind of people worship here? Who is their God?"[1]

King wonders, "Who is the Jesus these people are reading about in their Gospels?" Is he the same Jesus King follows? His faith points him toward a different interpretation of the role of the church, and he reminds his fellow Christian leaders of the context of the faith:

> *There was a time when the church was very powerful—in the time when the early Christians rejoiced at being deemed worthy to suffer for what they believed. In those days the church was not merely a thermometer that recorded the ideas and principles of popular opinion; it was a thermostat that transformed the mores of society. Whenever the early Christians entered a town, the people in power became disturbed and immediately sought to convict the Christians for being 'disturbers of the peace' and 'outside agitators.' But the Christians pressed on, in the conviction that they were 'a colony of heaven,' called to obey God rather than man. Small in number, they were big in commitment.[2]*

What was missing from under the roofs of those "lofty spires" was not good people with good intentions. King discusses how the biggest threat to the success of the civil rights movement was not the police or the Ku Klux Klan. It was all the nice, respectable church folks worshiping beneath those "lofty spires" who didn't want to get involved in such controversial matters. The real threat to change was those who knew what was right but valued their own peace and tranquility over the disruption required to achieve justice. The church was founded as "a colony of heaven," and participation in such a colony is neither safe nor predictable.

It's not uncommon in popular Christianity, to confuse or domesticate the mission of the Cross. If you interview most Christians today and ask them the purpose of Jesus's death and resurrection, you will likely get some version of the following: "Jesus came to forgive our sins so we can go to heaven when we die." While this may be true, Jesus's ultimate aim was far more provocative.

Jesus came to launch a revolution and to initiate the rebuilding of a new kingdom. He invaded this earth and planted a small "colony of heaven," not so a few believers could go to another heaven at some point, but so that, through his colony, he could remake this planet.

The Christian church was not to be the "thermometer of popular opinion," to quote King again; it was to be the "thermostat that transformed the mores of society." The message couldn't be more clear than when Jesus teaches his followers to pray, "Thy kingdom come, thy will be done on earth as it is in heaven." Jesus's ministry was an announcement that God's Kingdom was upon us. The restoration of creation had begun. In Jesus all things under heaven *and* earth are summed up. His story isn't just about a path to heaven. His story is the opening salvo of a rebellion against the principalities of the world. He came to reclaim that which was lost, and he intended to initiate this revolution through a new community of believers.

The safe and measured path is not the life promised by the Cross. Jesus offers far more than an insurance policy for the afterlife. The movement he launched was not intended to produce "nice," "compliant," "compromising" men and women. The "colony of heaven" is propelled forward by fierce, brave and selfless individuals committed to the notion that they are not on this earth to reflect the values of society but to shape them.

A Role to Play

In Part II of this book, we will turn our attention to the Hero's Journey Jesus is inviting us to take with him as our guide. Before wrapping up Part I, I want to set the stage for the adventure and provide the proper context for understanding the mission and its stakes. What we believe about the setting of our quest will determine how we interpret its purpose in our lives and may influence the role we allow faith in Jesus to play. It's sometimes hard to believe we are being called to take part in an epic drama, to have a role in the remaking of a new heaven and new earth. There is a harmful narrative among some Christians that the greatest hope of Christians is to one day have their spirit snatched from their body and transported to a nebulous, ephemeral heavenly existence. This common narrative misses the point entirely. New Testament Bible scholar, N. T. Wright, says, "The 'goal' is not 'heaven,' but a renewed human vocation within God's renewed creation. This is what every biblical book from Genesis on is pointing toward."[3]

What is this renewed human vocation Wright refers to? We are told at the beginning of the Bible:

"So God created mankind in his own image,
in the image of God he created them;
male and female he created them." (Gen 1:27 NIV)

God designed man to be his image-bearer in creation. Our vocation is to reflect God in the world. Jesus's activity in the world allows us to reclaim our identity as those image-bearers. As we journey with Jesus, we become more human, not less. And, as we embrace that reclaimed identity that had been lost until God entered history as both a myth and fact, we are invited to "reign" alongside him. This is the mission of the Hero's Journey: to discover who we were designed to be from the beginning and to take our places in God's unfolding story.

Reigning alongside God as his image-bearer has tangible implications here and now. This is not symbolic theological language indicating a future existence. N. T. Wright points out that the mistranslation of John 18:36 (starting with the King James Version), "My kingdom is not **of** this world," has been quoted endlessly to show the folly of any kind of social, cultural or political "mission." But what Jesus really said was, "My kingdom is not **from** this world."[3] Jesus isn't saying his kingdom is some far-off place concerned with far-off matters. He is indicating that his authority comes from elsewhere but that his concerns are for things that matter now as well as in eternity. His kingdom is not just in heaven. His kingdom is on earth **and** in heaven.

We are destined to rule as image-bearers, and in each of our lives, we are already granted a certain sphere of influence to develop as apprentices to Jesus. He reminds us of our vocation when he says, "Is it not written in the law, 'I have said you are gods'?"(John 10:34 NIV) He is the big "G" in "God" and we, as the little "g" in "gods," are to work alongside him. Philosopher Dallas Willard wrote about what it means to bear God's image and to embrace the fullness of our design:

Here is a truth that reaches into the deepest part of what it
means to be a person ... that we are made to 'have dominion'

*within an appropriate domain of reality. This is the core of the
likeness or image of God in us and is the basis of the destiny for
which we were formed. We are, all of us, never-ceasing spiritual
beings with a unique eternal calling to count for good in God's
great universe.... In creating human beings God made them to
rule, to reign, to have dominion in a limited sphere. Only so can
they be persons.*[5]

As we walk the Hero's path, we are doing far more than remaking
our character, although this may be one result of a successful journey.
Being an image-bearer is not about behaving in a certain way or
avoiding sin; it's about restoring our inherent capacities to create and
rule. This is not a vocation left only to saints. It's not a journey that
begins after death. Each person has a role to play in establishing a
colony of heaven as Jesus works through his followers to reclaim all
that was lost—including you.

A Return from Exile

This setting of our Hero's Journey is not for the faint of heart. We
have no idea of the kind of powers of corruption aligned against us.
We live in the midst of a battle, and if we need proof, we can look at
what comes against the people we love. Look at what has come against
you. Carnage is all around, and it is not always the physical kind of
carnage, but the emotional and spiritual kind that is often just as
debilitating. This is not the arena of "nice guys and gals." The
revolution requires hardened warriors, who have character and are so
sure of their identity that they can withstand and overcome any
opposition that comes against them and those who dare to live as if the
kingdom of heaven will rule supreme on earth once more.

We are, like the first-century Jews, exiles in our own homeland.
The Jews believed they were the chosen people of the one true God.
Yet they faced generations of persecution and exile. The ones who
made it back to the Promised Land (after their exile in Babylon in the
fourth-century BC) were ruled over by pagan oppressors. How could
they, the chosen people, suffer this indignity of living as foreigners in
their homeland? They wondered when God would forgive them of

their sins, renew the temple and restore the kingdom once and for all. The Jewish heritage from which Jesus's ministry was launched was a heritage waiting for God to deliver them from their long exile and return them to the new Eden.

We look around at the stunning beauty of the world and we see the potentiality of Eden among us. Yet we don't live in paradise. Far from it. We are like the Jews in Palestine when Jesus came. We are like Adam and Eve in the Garden of Eden when God discovered their transgression; we are strangers in a familiar place. Much like Jesus's story, the Jewish experience is both historical and metaphorical. It's the journey of mankind, the answers sought by all mythology. It begs the question, "How will we return from exile so that we may experience the type of life we were designed to have from the beginning?" How can we get back to Eden?

This setting on earth is full of reminders about the way things should be. A sweeping mountain vista, the cooing of a newborn child, the joy of an unexpected moment of laughter with friends—experiences that are so profound that time stands still, feelings of love so deep that they know no fear. We frequently come across clues about the way things were intended to be. But how quickly those moments are interrupted by reminders that our struggle has not reached its final resolution.

Eden was lost, but the colony of heaven, the new Eden, is being fought for, and that is the setting of our Hero's Journey. What are we to do about it in the meantime? Jesus tells us, "Let anyone who is thirsty come to me and drink. Whoever believes in me, as Scripture has said, rivers of living water will flow from within them." (John 7:37-38 NIV) Jesus also says that the earth will be restored. We are invited to join the battle, to relaunch his kingdom and to take part in the ongoing creation of the new Eden. As we do so, Jesus says that rivers of living water will flow through those of us who believe in him, and within our hearts will be the greatest reality, the new Eden, even before the battle of heaven and earth has been finally won.

In fact, the battle for the human heart has already been won for those who want to drink from what Jesus is offering and follow him on the quest. The rest of creation will be restored in due course. But the kingdom from another world is made manifest through Jesus as he works through the hearts of his believers. Through him we may once again taste the sweet nectars of Eden, drink from its pure waters and find peace and joy in the unyielding love poured out there.

Eternity Is Upon Us

Chances are that when you hear the word *eternal*, you think of some infinite future measured in time. When those who have a modern scientific mind read about Jesus telling his disciples, "Truly, truly I tell you, he who believes in me has eternal life," (John 6:47 NIV) they conceive of a life that goes on forever. Time is understood as a defined sequence of events, so when they hear the word *eternal*, they are tempted to think of "eternal life" as some yet-to-be-realized future. In the Christian context, that yet-to-be-realized future is often assumed to begin after death—the promise of eternal life is some mysterious state of being that they enter into later.

We might reasonably wonder what our emergencies, to-do lists and appointments have to do with eternity? But the truth is that today, this very moment, is eternity. When Jesus says "eternal life," he is describing an experience that our modern consciousness struggles to comprehend. Our perceptions today are so bound by time that we don't have an English word that appropriately captures the original language and messianic context of Jesus's promise of eternal life. Eternal is not primarily concerned with the temporal (i.e., the past and future). The eternal experience is one that stands beyond time. When Jesus says "eternal life," he is not referring to a future condition; rather, he is referring to a better condition. The eternal is timeless. It has always existed and will always exist beyond the constraints of time. Jesus offers a bridge to experiencing the eternal, but that has as much to do with quality as duration.

The Hero's Journey we are about to begin is not the delayed life waiting for eternity to come. Eternity is upon us now if we choose to approach it. The present, says C. S. Lewis, "is the point where eternity and time touch."[6] A successful quest leads to a greater awareness of eternal realities despite temporal settings. It helps us become present to our own life. And this is no small feat to live presently while the great masses of humanity go forth in a dreamlike haze, consumed by what has already happened or might happen in the future. In their preoccupation with the past and future, they miss their real life and its eternal significance. The proper Hero's Journey prepares us to see the evolving story around us in its magnificence and opens our consciousness to the mystery of God's creation and his presence throughout creation.

Those who believe in Jesus as the perfect Hero's guide will find that the eternal life is one where "streams of living water will flow through them." (John 7:38 NIV) They will have more to offer because they will connect with experiences that transcend sensory perception. The result is humans who are more connected to their true desires, capable of rare depths of love and live in ways that inspire others. Perhaps rivers of living water will flow before we enter "eternity" because "eternity" is here and now. It's today, and God offers us his eternal presence that defies all our senses and certainly all of the constraints of our temporal nature. I venture that we can barely fathom the fruit of the eternal promise.

What the Hero's Journey Is Not

As we begin the Hero's Journey, some of us may encounter temptations from modern church culture which may seek to alter our mission. Before we move on to the description of the various phases of the Hero's Journey, I want to offer caution regarding what the Hero's Journey is not about. We will encounter people who won't understand the personal spiritual nature of the quest, and, although perhaps well meaning, may distract our efforts to become a heroic image-bearer.

Managing Sin

It's no mystery that the message of the Gospels has often been reduced to one of sin management. Author Henry Cloud says that if we walk into a church on Sunday, we are apt to hear a message that goes like this, "God is good; you are bad. Try harder." The Christian life becomes a life of "Thou Shall Nots." Dallas Willard had similar concerns: "History has brought us to the point where the Christian message is thought to be essentially concerned only with how to deal with sin: with wrongdoing or wrong-being and its effects. Life, our actual existence, is not included in what is now presented as the heart of the Christian message, or it is included only marginally. That is where we find ourselves today."[7]

This is hardly an inspiring context for us to live our life, and it's not the message or mission of Jesus either. The Hero's Journey may result in a life where sin has diminishing power, but that isn't the primary objective. It's a fallacy that imprisons us in a tiny and frustrating story. Sin is a problem of the will, but the will is not changed or subdued by us trying harder. It's an illogical argument to say that our problem is a corruption of the will and then propose a solution that suggests that we can overcome the corruption of the will by using it more. It doesn't work or make sense, but yet it remains a popular message in church circles.

Jesus already dealt with sin once and for all. For those who accept his grace, all past, present and future sin are not only forgiven but also forgotten—and we are a new creation. If we make sin management our mission, we are ignoring this fundamental promise. The solution to overcoming the corruption of the will is the remaking of the will altogether. This is the process of the Hero's Journey: a remaking of our will as we find alignment with our original design and core desires. This is how sin comes under the mastery of the Hero—not by intensifying our efforts but by surrendering to a larger purpose and, in doing so, allowing a higher power to remake the will.

Sin is symptomatic of disconnection and a reflection of our will apart from its intended purpose. To treat the problem of sin without addressing its underlying cause can, at best, lead to only temporary relief. Holiness doesn't come as a result of guilt, shame and sin accountability programs. Holiness comes as a result of the Hero being reconstituted and returned from his exile. A mission objective to behave better and to sin less is doomed to failure.

Justice Movements

I began this chapter discussing Martin Luther King, Jr.'s call for the white moderates within the churches in the South to come to the aid of the civil rights movement. But it's important to distinguish between the Hero's Journey and a justice movement. King observed that the early Christians were "small in number but big in commitment." They disrupted the status quo because they had the courage of their convictions. They wouldn't back down when things got hard, just as King didn't, even though their beliefs might result in great personal risk.

The point of the Hero's quest is to prepare normal people for whatever adventure or cause they find Jesus drawing them toward. The best leaders and examples for a justice movement, the people who will most likely struggle through when the justice movement becomes difficult, inconvenient or is no longer venerated, will be the ones who have been simultaneously remade by their personal quest.

Certainly, living within a larger story today may point us toward helping to relieve the world of hunger, sex trafficking or other human rights violations. Solving these issues reflects an understanding of a quest that is bigger than how much money we can put in our bank account. If we are involved in one of these missions, we should be commended for our efforts to alleviate others' suffering. But social justice isn't the only outcome of the Hero's quest.

In addition, let no one deceive us that a just cause or service will replace the transforming work that Jesus wants to do in our life. We don't want to sell ourselves short. We will make the greatest impact when we engage in each of those justice missions as a well-journeyed Hero who knows who he is because he has faced the trials and has emerged victorious on the other side. The hero is the person who has the faith, abilities and assurance to transform an ordinary movement into a truly inspired one.

Self-Indulgent Adventure

The Hero's quest is not an excuse for self-indulgent adventure. As we will see, the Hero who is being transformed may experience transcendent highs and may develop a reluctance to reengage in his normal working world. If he isn't careful, the quest may become an idol itself and he may forget that his mission is to bring his gifts to the people in his life, especially those who are closest to him.

Any journey that ends with the Hero neglecting his greatest sphere of influence, his family, in the name of some greater mission is a fallacy. It is emblematic of a Hero who has not reached maturity. It's not rare within influential movements that a leader's children and spouse come to understand their position as secondary and subservient to the movement. This situation might work for a time, but then the movement often gets derailed when personal emergencies in the leader's life can no longer go ignored.

The proper Hero views the quest not as something he does for himself but as something he does for the benefit of his family, friends and community. He balances the adventures that captivate his desires and getting caught up in something profound within the reality of his domain of responsibility. Too many people live as if nothing is going on outside their own story. The Hero understands the difference and doesn't allow the adventure to become a small story itself. Even noble causes can undermine an untrained hero if the motive for doing great work devolves into one of self-gratification and self-promotion.

Getting Started

In his book, *Road to Character*, journalist David Brooks examines the lives of a dozen inspiring leaders in history who, through internal struggles and a sense of their own limitations, built rare strength of character. He concludes that modern culture's obsession with self-promotion and moral relativism has harmful consequences on the individual, resulting in a person with the following character:

> *... You don't have a clear idea of the sources of meaning in life, so you don't know where you should devote your skills, which career path will be highest and best. Years pass and the deepest parts of yourself go unexplored and unstructured. You are busy, but you have a vague anxiety that your life has not achieved its ultimate meaning and significance. You live with an unconscious*

boredom, not really loving, not really attached to the moral purposes that give life its worth. You lack the internal criteria to make unshakable commitments. You never develop inner constancy, the integrity that can withstand popular disapproval or a serious blow. You find yourself doing things that other people approve of, whether these things are right for you or not. You foolishly judge other people by their abilities, not by their worth. You do not have a strategy to build character, and without that, not only your inner life but also your external life will eventually fall to pieces.[8]

We might think of "character" as referring to how we act, but "character" is more about the quality and integrity of our nature. The Hero's Journey is a strategy for building character because it reconnects us with our intended design. It's about discovering our true identity instead of living with a fictitious identity that we create in order to promote ourselves. The well-journeyed Hero knows who he is, and his character is grounded in that understanding.

Why is finding fulfillment in life so difficult for most people? Why is discovering life's purpose so elusive? I think we are tempted into believing that happiness or fulfillment will come by changing our circumstances. We think, "I will be happy once I can find the right career"; "I will feel fulfilled by taking up a new hobby"; "I will feel complete when I have the right romantic relationship." Then our circumstances change, and somehow the same haunting questions remain. The issue is we are solving the wrong problem. The problem is not the wrong job, wrong spouse or wrong hobby. The starting point for the answers we seek and the means to fulfilling the desires we can't even name is a more fundamental question. First we must answer the question, "Who am I?" This is what the Hero's Journey is intended to reveal, and by giving us a sense of who we are, we begin directing our attention to the things that we ought to do with our lives.

To experience the eternal quality of life, to see the new Eden in the midst of the sin and chaos of the modern world, we have to take Jesus's journey. Not literally of course, but as Jesus suggests: "If anyone would come after me, let him deny himself and take up his cross and follow me. For whoever would save his life will lose it, but whoever loses his life for my sake will find it." (Mark 8:34 NIV) It's what every hero faces: losing his old identity in order to find a new and better one. Taking up the Cross indicates the sacrifice required. It involves the suffocation of the Hero's instinct for self-preservation and the triumph over his greatest fears. The Hero must cross the First Threshold, enter the Belly of the Whale, emerge to face trials and tribulations, find Atonement with the Father and, in the end, be remade into the Hero that the kingdom of heaven and earth requires in order to advance the revolution begun on a Cross outside Jerusalem. Let us begin that quest.

PART II

For the duration of this book, we will cover the various phases of the Hero's Journey in detail. In Chapter II, I summarized each sub-act of the journey, and for reference I will include the relevant summary before discussing each phase. As we consider each phase in Part II, I will highlight the parallels to popular movies. I could have chosen hundreds of titles that use the Hero's Journey framework. I tried to choose movies I thought would be familiar to most readers and in which all the phases of the Hero's Journey are particularly explicit. Since the Hero's Journey is not gender-limited, I also sought representation from both a male and female perspective. I will continue to use the term "Hero" as a non-gender-specific designation.

CHAPTER VII

CALL TO ADVENTURE

The Hero's Journey begins with a Call to Adventure in which some information is received that beckons the Hero to leave the mundane normalcy of his current surroundings and venture into the unknown. The call brings a new awareness to the Hero and draws him into relation with forces he doesn't quite understand. Sometimes the Journey is introduced by a "Herald"—a symbolic or literal figure summoning the Hero to look beyond his current circumstances and understanding about the world around him. In some cases the Hero is called to the adventure because of a crisis created by his own shortcomings or the shortcomings of others. At other times he is enticed from the common path of life by some interesting phenomenon. Sometimes the Hero is set on his Journey by the will of another. Often what the Hero values and cherishes begins to shift as he becomes aware that much of what he thinks is real is, in fact, an illusion. As the truth about reality becomes apparent, he becomes aware of a new destiny. The Hero will quickly recognize that the Call to Adventure will require much of him. It will require him to change, to adapt and to allow himself to be transfigured in order to accomplish his mission.

JESUS WAS THIRTY YEARS OLD when he arrived at the Jordan River to be baptized by his cousin John. From there he headed out into the wilderness and was tempted by the devil for forty days, and when he returned, he launched his ministry to change the world. I have sometimes wondered why Jesus chose the particular day he did to set out on his adventure. What was going through his mind and for how many months or years had he stood at his carpenter's workbench in Nazareth contemplating his future mission?

Jesus's parents knew of the unique circumstances of his birth, but what other clues suggested that he would launch a movement that would change the world forever? He lived in a small village in the northern hills of Galilee, worked in the family business and led the life of a typical first-century Jew. Then, one day, thirty years into his life, he heeds the Call to Adventure, puts down his tools and heads out toward the wilderness in preparation to become the Hero of all Heroes.

Just like Jesus's story, all the best stories start in an ordinary world. The Hero lives in a sleepy town, works at a regular job and has normal family responsibilities. He doesn't stand out in the world. His life doesn't seem remarkable. Then one day the Hero has an inkling that things are not all they seem to be. The clues come to the Hero in countless ways. He becomes aware that something is missing—that what he believes is real, is not. Perhaps he realizes something has been taken from him that he must recover, or an important task is set upon him that he cannot ignore. He is called into the adventure. Screenwriters describe the Call to Adventure as an "inciting incident," the trigger for moving the story forward. It's when the Hero's Ordinary World is interrupted: the princess is kidnapped, the war is launched or a messenger arrives.

Calls from the Big Screen

During the day Thomas Anderson is a programmer for a large, respectable software company, but he spends most of his spare time as a computer hacker operating under the alias "Neo." During his illicit hacking operations, Neo discovers references to a vague concept known as "the Matrix," which Neo believes might explain the strange sense he has felt his entire life "that something is wrong with the world." Neo spends years searching for the one person who can explain the Matrix to him, a supposed terrorist known as Morpheus.

Working in his cubicle one day, Neo receives a package. He opens it to find a cell phone inside. As Neo looks closely at the phone, it begins to ring. Neo hesitates but finally answers. A man on the other end of the phone identifies himself as Morpheus, and he tells Neo he is going to show him the reality of the ordinary world he thinks he is living in. Neo has received his Call to Adventure.

You may recognize this plot from the movie the *Matrix*. Neo is one of billions of humans who unknowingly exist in a simulated reality. The Matrix is a computer program hooked into the brains of humans to deceive them about the sinister reality of their existence. They think they are living in a normal world, but they are not aware of the true state of their existence as prisoners being harvested for their energy-generating powers; in reality, they reside in small transparent liquid-filled pods.

Luke Skywalker lives with his aunt and uncle on a remote and desolate planet named Tatooine. They are moisture farmers living in the middle of a desert. One day Luke and his uncle purchase a pair of damaged droids from a scavenger clan of Jawas. While cleaning the sand out of the newly acquired droid, called R2D2, Luke discovers a holographic distress message from a woman identifying herself as Princess Leia. She is trying to reach a man named Obi-wan-kenobi proclaiming he is her only hope.

Luke finds the old hermit Ben Kenobi, who lives up in the hills near Luke's home, and shows him the encoded message. After seeing the message from Princess Leia, Kenobi asks Luke to accompany him to the planet Alderaan and let him teach Luke about the Force. Luke, a young man living an ordinary life, far away from the spheres of power and influence in the universe, has received his Call to Adventure. An unlikely Hero given his circumstances and upbringing, little does Luke know that his journey to restore the balance of the Force throughout the universe and lead a rebellion against the evil galactic empire is about to begin.

Recognizing the Call

The Call to Adventure can best be summarized as a deep, incessant desire mixed with a healthy dose of fear and uncertainty that disrupts the equilibrium of your life. Answering the call may mean moving to a new city or starting a new career. It may involve writing a book, recording a podcast or speaking to an audience. It may require working on your marriage or addressing an addiction. The list of possible adventures are endless. Other examples include working on your own heart to recover from past wounds that have paralyzed your spiritual and emotional growth, embarking on a creative project, launching a new business, starting a new ministry, taking time off, sacrificing a prized hobby, letting go of possession(s) or way of life, fighting for your health or beginning a new relationship.

The first step in the Hero's Journey is to recognize when one of these adventures is calling you. It will not be as obvious as a terrorist named Morpheus mailing you a cell phone at work or receiving a holographic message from a princess. The call comes in more subtle ways. Some Hero's Journeys begin with a positive affirmation. An experience, a book or a message you hear may uplift and inspire you. You may sense a stirring in your heart that can no longer be ignored. Some influential person, real or fictitious, may enter your life and help you see truths you couldn't see before.

At other times the Call to Adventure comes when an Ordinary World gets disrupted. While this is not the most desirable way to start your journey, it is sometimes the only way we ever have enough motivation to change. We may lose a job or an important relationship, or we may experience a health scare or some other existential crisis shocks us out of our stupor. Many people make peace with living in the "Matrix," and while we may sense there should be more to life, our heart may be too numb to do anything about it until a painful disruption blindsides us and forces us to consider a new path—or gives us no better alternative.

Not every injury is a Call to Adventure, but events that come as a complete disruption to our ordinary world should be a reason to pause and think. When our plan for life goes awry, it may be because a better destiny awaits us. The temptation might be to try to fix things as quickly as possible, to numb away disappointment or to double down on efforts to organize life the way we want it. But if we ignore the call, it will continue to reemerge. Circumstances may change, but underlying problems won't go away. When we feel disoriented by events in our lives or the same problem keeps repeating itself and our coping strategies keep breaking down, it may be time to consider a different approach. An important invitation may await us.

The good news is that we don't have to wait for a disruptive event to find clues about the adventure awaiting us. Our deepest desires are navigational beacons, drawing us through the dangerous fog toward the adventures intended to save us. Moments of inspiration and wonder may serve as reminders of those desires. Sometimes we can't escape a gnawing sense that we need to take a step in a new direction or that we are missing out on some meaningful adventure. If we choose to take the risk, we can enter the adventure on our own terms and follow our unique gifting and desires (instead of pain and disappointment) into the realm of the unknown.

As an example, this book is the beginning of a personal Hero's Journey. I am not a writer by trade, an academic or a professional minister, but for five years I have had a desire to write this book. I have dabbled with writing but never had the time to do so consistently. My desire remained muddled, so I never took the risk to commit the time and emotional energy toward the writing process. I would often get started writing about an idea, but life would get busy and I wouldn't think about writing for several weeks. Still, the desire just wouldn't go away and kept resurfacing in different, unexpected ways.

I remember the moment I decided to answer this particular Call to Adventure. I was listening to a podcast while commuting home from work. At the end of the podcast, the host answered a few questions sent in from his audience. The host is a successful author, so one member of the audience asked about his writing process. He talked about how difficult writing was for him and the toll each book took on him. Then he said something that really struck me: "You should only write a book if it will be more painful not to write it." That was the Call to Adventure for me.

I should say more accurately, this wasn't the only Call to Adventure. In reality I had been ignoring invitations for five years. Odd little coincidences and moments of inspiration would crop up in seemingly connected ways. I would randomly stumble upon a book like Joseph Campbell's, *A Hero with a Thousand Faces*, or a friend would make an offhand comment and, with no knowledge or intent, remind me of my desire. Random ideas from disparate sources (books, conversations, movies, articles) would came together like a giant jigsaw puzzle in my mind.

If I had listened to the podcast a year earlier, I don't know whether it would have had the same impact on me. I suspect it wouldn't. The reason it had an impact on me the way it did is because it articulated exactly the way I felt about writing. Every time the desire to write this book came up and I didn't answer it, I felt like I was missing out on something. With each ignored call, I experienced a small twinge of regret, each one building on the previous one. The internal dissonance reached the point at which, because of one particular comment, I realized it would be more painful not to write this book than it would be to write it, and that was the final confirmation I needed.

I don't know where this particular Hero's Journey is heading for me, but I know uncertainty is inherent in the adventure. If I knew the outcome before I started, it wouldn't make for much of a story. Every Hero's Journey requires risk. I don't know if people will ever read this book (except you mom and dad), and if they do, I don't know how they will receive it. So, in sharing my thoughts in this book with the world, there is the possibility of rejection, which feels risky. Also, when I answered the call, the first tangible step required that I change some priorities. I realized writing could no longer be something I got around to whenever I had time or felt like writing. I had to put this project at the top of my list and drop other things further down. I am a small business owner, but I decided that for a season this project would come before my business and livelihood. For now I have chosen to start each day writing, and therefore I ignore the e-mails stacking up in my in-box. I am continually challenged with self-doubt about the wisdom of my priorities and my abilities in this arena.

We might recognize our own adventures because they won't be comfortable. And just because something appears to be adventurous or noble doesn't mean it's a Call to Adventure. The Hero's Journey shouldn't serve as an excuse to run away from disappointment or fear. Some missions seem altruistic and risky to outsiders, but only the would-be Hero knows the truth—whether the true motive of the endeavor is to delay facing something truly risky and difficult. The Hero's Journey doesn't perpetuate masks and false identities; it reveals the authentic person. The ultimate purpose of the journey is not for ourselves alone either. It will serve a larger purpose in our lives, but it should reflect a purpose in the lives of others as well, especially those closest to us.

Synchronicity and Other Terms

Swiss psychologist Carl Jung coined the term "synchronicity" to describe coincidental events that on the surface have no explainable connection but seem to relate to some deeper reality. The following are some examples. You go to a bookstore and for no reason pick up a book, flip randomly to a page and see an answer to a question that you had been asking yourself when you walked into the store. You experience financial difficulty, but somehow money for basic living expenses shows up at just the right time and the bills get paid. You think about calling a particular person to ask for advice on something important, and in the midst of your thought, the person calls you. Almost all of us have had similar experiences. They are ones when we say, "What a coincidence!"

Jung believed coincidental "acausal" events, like the ones just described, couldn't be explained by statistics. The probabilities didn't add up. Jung concluded that many of the experiences perceived as coincidences reflected a deeper governing dynamic at work in the world, which he labeled "the collective unconscious." "Synchronicity" was his term for explaining that the world and our personality manifest clues that direct our attention and actions. Most of the time, we dismiss these events as mere coincidence (a statistical anomaly), but according to Jung, this can't always result from chance. Jung thought we should give credence to connected coincidental events because they might be clues that the universe and our own subconscious were working together to get our attention and to move us in a new direction.

In an interview shortly before his death, Joseph Campbell spoke about a similar concept by summarizing an essay by famed philosopher Arthur Schopenhauer, called the "Apparent Intention of Fate of an Individual." Campbell, speaking in the interview, said:

> (Schopenhauer) points out that when you reach an advanced age and look back over your lifetime, it can seem to have had a consistent order and plan, as though composed by some novelist. Events that when they occurred had seemed accidental and of little moment turn out to have been indispensable factors in the composition of a consistent plot.... The whole thing gears together like one big symphony, with everything unconsciously structuring everything else. Schopenhauer concluded that it is as though our lives were the features of the one great dream of a single dreamer in which all the dream characters dream, too; so that everything links to everything else, moved by the one will to life which is the universal will in nature. [1]

What Schopenhauer labeled "fate," what Jung labeled "synchronicity" and what Campbell labeled "consciousness," I label "God's activity in his creation," which he initiates through the work of his Holy Spirit. In his letter to the Romans, Paul writes: "The spirit helps us in our weakness. We do not know what we ought to pray for, but the Spirit himself intercedes for us through wordless groans." (Rom 8:26 NIV) Even when we don't know what we want or what is best for us, when we don't even know what we should be praying for, "The Spirit intercedes for God's people in accordance with the will of God."(Rom 8:27 NIV)

Even skeptics like Schopenhauer and Jung noticed that sometimes there seems to be an intention for what is happening in our lives. Events that seem random and unconnected may, in fact, be important and formative turning points. The Call to Adventure is constantly revealing itself, begging us to cooperate with the "single dreamer." Some calls are hard to miss; others emerge through a trail of coincidental events and chance meetings. Some come as a manifestation of a deep desire, and some come out of disappointment. But the Hero has a choice—to heed the call to Adventure or not. God is always moving in the world, and his eyes "range throughout the earth to strengthen those whose hearts are fully committed to him." (2 Chron 16:9 NIV) Everyone gets the call but not everyone answers.

Refusal of the Call

The Hero has a choice right away: to answer the call or not. In many cases the Hero may turn away from the adventure. He may refuse out of duty and responsibility to his Ordinary World. Often he will feel reluctance because of fear or feelings of inadequacy. He may sense what lies beyond the pale and may not want to depart from the comforts of his surroundings and his way of life. And though he may succeed in building upon his kingdom and comfortable way of life, his refusal to answer the call robs him of his power. By refusing the call he may get what he wants, but in getting it he also becomes a victim. The life and story he wants to control, in the end, control him. Sometimes the Hero will initially refuse the call but with further guidance or upon reflection may reconsider.

Choosing to answer the Call to Adventure is an important step because it's far from a given and many Heroes hesitate at first. Fear often stops a would-be Hero in his tracks. In fact, any time we are wondering if we should take a step and need clarification about whether a particular event is a Call to Adventure or a distraction, fear may be a good indicator that an adventure is awaiting.

One reason fear accompanies the Call to Adventure is that the Hero intuitively understands that the adventure will require something of him that he doesn't know whether he is prepared to give. He wonders if he really has the substance to make it through the ordeal and is haunted by the question, "Do I have what it takes?" Even the most assured Hero will encounter adventures that will make him doubt the answer. To deal with the fear (and ignore the call), the Hero makes up excuses such as "I will get to that task later when I have time" (which he never does) or "I have responsibilities, and pursuing this adventure would be irresponsible." Sometimes the Hero just dismisses the call outright, reasoning that he is not the person for the task. He excuse himself, citing a lack of credentials, knowledge, skills or another factor.

In our own life, we might relate to what Luke says when the old hermit Ben Kenobi asks Luke to accompany him to Alderaan and to let him teach Luke the ways of the force. Luke says, "I can't get involved! I've got work to do. It's not that I like the Empire ... I hate it. But there's nothing I can do about it right now." This sounds like all the nice church folks we talked about in the previous chapter. It sounds like all of us at different times in our lives, reasoning that we need to get back to work and let someone more capable do the hard work that matters.

In the epic poem the *Divine Comedy*, Dante tries to refuse his adventure with another common excuse. As the *Divine Comedy* begins, Dante, the pilgrim, is heading for a tour of the afterlife when he looks toward his guide, Virgil, and asks, "But I, why should I go there, and who grants it? I am not Aeneas; I am not Paul. Neither I nor any man thinks me fit for this, so that if I commit myself to go I fear lest my going be folly." Dante compares himself to his heroes, Aeneas and Paul, pointing out that he is not like them. He claims he doesn't have their substance of character, so the journey in which he is about to embark feels like a mistake. This is standard logic when refusing the call; we don't dare compare ourselves to more prominent people. We conclude that they have a superior trait or a unique calling and we don't. In reality, the critical difference between us and those Heroes to whom we dare not compares ourselves is that they heeded the call and we doubt the wisdom of doing the same.

The second reason fear accompanies the Call to Adventure is that the Hero recognizes that, in order to make it through the journey, he will have to make a sacrifice he isn't sure he wants to make. The Hero has to give something up, which almost always will be experienced as losing part of himself. No journey comes without a cost. If the point of the Hero's Journey is to be remade into something new and better, then the Hero must die to his old way of life. "Refusal (of the Call to Adventure) is essentially a refusal to give up what one takes to be one's own interest," said Joseph Campbell.

I refused the Call to Adventure for five years before I started on this book because I wanted to write it without taking any risk. Overcoming these initial fears is part of the purpose of the journey. When we get to the end of a successful quest, we will find that our fear has lost its power over us, but in the midst of the journey, hesitation and doubt are inherent and timeless struggles for every Hero.

Even Jesus experienced moments of doubt. In the Garden of Gethsemane he prays throughout the night, knowing the time has come and he will soon be taken, tried and crucified. He prays, "My Father, if it is possible, may this cup be taken from me." (Mt 26:39 NIV) He is anguished at the prospect of the hours to come. Often God just wants small sacrifices from us, and they scare us to death. Jesus was going to pay the ultimate price. He continues his prayer though: ... "Yet not as I will, but as you will." He is aligning his story with the will of the Father. The agony and pain he will endure cannot compare to the glory to come.

Paul says the same thing may be expected for all of God's image-bearing heroes: "I consider that our present sufferings are not worth comparing with the glory that will be revealed in us. For the creation waits in eager expectation for the children of God to be revealed." (Romans 8:18 NIV) God promises that the fruit of the journey is worth the risk and that all of the fear and uncertainty and even suffering we may experience will find a new perspective one day. And we will see it was not even worth comparing to the bounty received.

I should also point out that in real life, the Call to Adventure may often go ignored because the Hero isn't even aware he is being called. He refuses without even knowing it. He misses all the signs and signals despite how obvious they may be to everyone else. There is a great sequence in the movie *Bruce Almighty* that articulates in a clever and humorous way the tragic reality of the kind of lack of awareness that far too many people live with.

In the movie the main character, Bruce (played by Jim Carrey), experiences the worst day of his life. He loses his job to a rival, gets beat up after trying to help a homeless man and ends up in a huge fight with his girlfriend. In desperation Bruce goes for a drive and prays to God for guidance on what to do.

"Send me a sign, God," he prays, and a road sign flashes "Caution Ahead."

He doesn't notice the flashing sign and continues his prayer, "Send me a signal, God," and a truck pulls in front of him, and it's full of "Stop" signs, "Caution" signs, "Do Not Enter" signs and "Dead End" signs.

Bruce becomes annoyed by the slow-moving truck in front of him and speeds past it. He grabs his girlfriend's prayer beads hanging from the rearview mirror and prays, "Please, God, reach into my life...." He hits a pothole and drops the beads to the floor of the car. As Bruce reaches down to grab them, he loses control and slams into a light pole. In frustration and anger, he gets out of the mangled car and yells toward the heavens, "Smite me, Almighty smiter." He throws the prayer beads into the river, and as the scene closes, Bruce screams at God, "Answer me!" God was trying to answer, but Bruce wasn't listening.

We may know someone like Bruce. Everyone sees they are about to drive into a light pole but them. They won't heed wise and loving counsel. They won't take enough time to self-reflect on how their decisions are impacting their own heart, or they try to self-reflect but can't be honest with themselves. It should be obvious that if they don't consider a different path forward, they will destroy their health, marriage, career or life. Yet they have somehow come to view the messages and signs the way Bruce did in the movie, as annoyances and obstacles to be overcome and explained away.

In today's culture it's easy to live in a small story with an egocentric view of the universe, in complete lack of awareness of the stories being told outside of our own. In the process we may not even be aware of the persistent calls to take a new direction. This is a problem for Christians and non-Christians alike. Many people worship God on Sunday but live the other six days of the week as practical agnostics. Or they live at the other extreme, which we discussed in the previous chapter, so that the adventure of the Gospel gets reduced to behavior techniques and managing sin. This is just another self-centered story but with religious drapery that sends the non-Christians running for the hills when it comes to what is being portrayed as the Gospel.

In mythology the persistent refusal of the Call to Adventure leads to tragedy. In the real world, it does too, but not always in the sense we think of as tragic. In some cases like the Bruce Almighty's of the world, it can certainly lead to professional and personal hardship that we can identify as tragic. In other cases the people get exactly what they want—a secure job, a compliant spouse, a big house, a nice pension, luxurious vacations, and so forth…. But the real tragedy is that every time they ignore the Call to Adventure, a little part of them dies. One day they get to a point in their lives where they look back and wonder what it was all for—all the hard work, the years of service, the energy they poured out. Why did they do it? They retire and realize they don't know the person staring back at them in the mirror. They have numerous acquaintances but no deep and meaningful relationships. Their spouse tolerates them, but intimacy has been lost forever. They have great résumés, but nobody knows what to say about them at their funeral. This is the real tragedy of ignoring the repeated Calls to Adventure.

Adventures Big and Small

In the real world some Hero's Journeys last a week while others last a lifetime. Some journeys seem innocuous while others are matters of life and death. The Hero's Journey is not a one-time event; it's an endless cycle leading to increasingly greater maturity and self-awareness. At times a real-world Hero may embark on multiple journeys simultaneously. At first he may not even notice the connection between the various adventures he's had throughout his life. But as Schopenhauer suggested, he will come to a point where he will look back and see how all the adventures come together into a coherent narrative. One day they will all make sense, and he will understand how his personal journey with all of its sub-acts fits into God's universal story.

So, as we venture forth on our journey, accepting the calls placed in front of us, we would do well to remember "that in all things God works for the good of those who love him, who have been called according to his purpose." (Rom 8:28 NIV) In the next chapter, we will meet our SuperNatural aid who will accompany us as we depart our Ordinary World.

CHAPTER VIII

SUPERNATURAL AID

The Adventure will require too much of the Hero for him to make it on his own accord. The stakes are too high, and the Hero will need to be fortified and reassured. Once the Hero becomes committed to the quest, a SuperNatural aid will appear as a guide and protector along the journey, a figure who not only helps direct the Hero's path but also puts the forces of nature and destiny at the hero's side.

JOHN THE BAPTIST WORKED out on the frontier by the Jordan River. He was a wild man who lived off the land, fed himself with locusts and honey, and dressed in primitive clothes. The people came from all over the countryside of Judea to hear John preach and confess their sins before being baptized in the river. He told the crowds coming to him each day: "I baptize you with water for repentance. But after me comes one who is more powerful than I, whose sandals I am not worthy to carry. He will baptize you with the Holy Spirit and fire." (Matt 3:11 NIV)

Then one day Jesus arrived to be baptized. Recognizing the significance, John hesitated, concerned that the moment was too big for him. But Jesus convinced him otherwise, and John lowered Jesus under the slow-moving water of the Jordan River. The scriptures say, "As soon as Jesus was baptized, he went up out of the water. At that moment heaven was opened, and he saw the Spirit of God descending like a dove and alighting on him. And a voice from heaven said, "This is my Son, whom I love; with him I am well pleased." (Matt 3:16-17 NIV)

This episode marked the beginning of Jesus's ministry. As we discussed in the previous chapter, Jesus lived for thirty years before he entered the field of adventure that would cast him as the savior of the world. When he met John the Baptist, he had not yet performed a miracle. He had no followers. He was a carpenter from the small village of Nazareth. But then Jesus came to the point in his life where he was ready to begin his Hero's Journey, and he needed a helper to accompany him. He required the Spirit of God, which descended on him like a dove.

The scriptures say that after his baptism, Jesus went into the wilderness "full of the Spirit." (Lk 4:1 NIV) The Spirit walked with Jesus through the trials and temptations he faced during his forty days beyond the Jordan River. The Spirit empowered his ministry and equipped Jesus with the gifts required to fulfill his mission. It was through the Spirit that Jesus performed his miracles. It was through the Spirit that Jesus asserted his authority over Satan. He preached by the Spirit, healed by the Spirit and led by the Spirit. Jesus's human nature needed to be inspired by an external power, and throughout the Gospels he reminded his followers that it was through God, the Father, working with the Spirit that Jesus accomplished the many feats that so amazed the people. He explained to them, "God gives the Spirit without limit." Jesus, the Hero, could not complete his mission alone—even Jesus required a SuperNatural aid.

From the Big Screen

In fictional stories the SuperNatural aid may be symbolized in various ways. A mentor with mystical powers may fulfill the role. Sometimes the Hero is given a weapon or tool engendered with extraordinary powers. It could be nature herself that breaks into the narrative to assist in the Hero's quest. They all have the same function—to keep the Hero on his path when the powers against the Hero threaten to break him.

In the movie *The Wizard of Oz,* the quintessential Hero, Dorothy, is whirled up in a tornado from inside her uncle and aunt's house. When the house comes crashing down and Dorothy goes to the door, she realizes she isn't in Kansas anymore. She wonders if the place in which she now stands is "somewhere over the rainbow," but she quickly discovers she is now in Munchkin-Land, a region in the World of Oz. The first person she encounters in this mysterious world is the good witch, Glinda, who will help guide Dorothy through her journey. It is Glinda who points Dorothy toward Oz and provides her with the knowledge about how the mystical world of Oz works. She intervenes to save Dorothy when the wicked witch uses a field of poppies to lure Dorothy into a deep slumber. It's Glinda who reveals to Dorothy that she has always had the ability to get home and instructs her to click her ruby slippers together and repeat "there is no place like home."

In *The Lord of the Rings* trilogy by J.R.R. Tolkien, the unlikely Hero is Frodo, a Hobbit living in a quiet, peaceful region of Middle-earth known as the Shire. Frodo is brought into his own Hero's Journey when he comes into possession of his Uncle Bilbo's mysterious and powerful ring. Gandalf, a wise old wizard and friend of his uncle, explains to Frodo the history of the ring and its potential to do enormous harm should it fall into the hands of its original owner, a diabolical creature named Sauron. To defeat Sauron the ring must be returned to where it had been forged inside the Mountain of Doom, deep in the territory of Mordor, and destroyed in the molten lava flowing through it.

Gandalf serves as Frodo's SuperNatural aid during his quest. Gandalf organizes a fellowship of heroes to accompany Frodo on the first part of his journey to Mordor. When Frodo and the fellowship of the ring travels through the caves of Moria, Gandalf fights the giant fiery dragon creature called Balrog, making it possible for the group to escape the caves. At the end of the series, with his mission complete, Frodo and his his friend Sam find themselves stranded on an outcropping of rock amid a sea of volcanic lava. When it appears that this will be the end for Frodo and Sam, Gandalf arrives with three giant eagles and rescues them.

In one of the most memorable exchanges in *The Lord of the Rings* series, Gandalf offers Frodo the encouragement and wisdom he needs to continue. Frodo is exhausted by his burden of carrying the ring and is near the point of giving up.

Frodo: *I wish the ring had never come to me. I wish none of this had happened.*

Gandalf: *So do all who live to see such times. But that is not for them to decide. All we have to decide is what to do with the time that is given to us. There are other forces at work in this world, Frodo, besides the will of evil. Bilbo was meant to find the ring, in which case you also were meant to have it. And that is an encouraging thought.*

What Gandalf tells Frodo is no less true for us. We have a decision to make on how we shall live our lives, and an important question will be whether we will take encouragement in the belief that there may be forces at work in our world supporting the destiny intended for each one of us.

Ordinary Folks Doing Extraordinary Things

What do we do if we don't have a paternal wizard or a fairy godmother show up to guide us? For some help answering this question, I want to turn to The Acts of the Apostles. For reference, the book of Acts is the one that follows the four Gospels in the New Testament. It's written by the same person who wrote the Gospel of Luke. In fact, Luke and Acts form a two-part narrative. The first part chronicles Jesus's ministry leading up to his death and resurrection. The second part chronicles the ministry of the early Church following Jesus's departure.

The book of Acts contains a stunning collection of stories about the undaunted courage of the first Christians and the miraculous acts that transpired through the work of the early Christian Church. The most prominent feature of these stories is the participation of the "Holy Spirit." It's been said that the book of Acts could very well have been called the Gospel of the Holy Spirit. In the American Standard Version of Acts, "Spirit" is mentioned fifty-six times and makes clear that the heroes of the early days of the "movement" depended on "being full of the Holy Spirit" to do God's work.

In the first few lines of Acts, Jesus lays out the central theme for the entire ministry of the early church. He tells his apostles that their SuperNatural aid will be coming to help them soon: "You will receive power when the Holy Spirit comes on you; and you will be my witnesses in Jerusalem, and in all Judea and Samaria, and to the ends of the earth." (Acts 1:8 NIV) Their mission is to tell the entire world about Jesus, and their success depends on the Holy Spirit.

Take Peter as an example of the extent of this external power. He is one of the prominent figures of the early church, and his transformation provides a remarkable juxtaposition between the Peter found in Part I of the story, captured by the Gospels, and the Peter found in

Part II, captured in the book of Acts. It's like reading about two different people. Peter enters the biblical narrative as an ordinary fisherman who drops everything to follow Jesus. And while Jesus predicts that Peter will be the rock on which God will build his church, Peter has troubling character flaws. Peter can be impulsive, stubborn and lazy. He is sometimes slow to catch on to what Jesus has taught him, and on more than one occasion, must be reprimanded for his petulance. In the face of his most critical trial, Peter fails not once but three times—denying Jesus just as Jesus warned him that he would.

When we meet Peter in the second part of the story, beginning after Jesus's ascension to heaven, what we encounter is a Heroic character—confident, inspirational and courageous—transformed and fully committed to his quest. In his first public address about Jesus, Peter's words have such authority that 3,000 people immediately convert. He passes by people, and they are healed by his shadow. In one story Peter and John (another Apostle) are teaching the people when they are arrested by the Jewish religious leaders and rulers who feel threatened by the spread of Christianity. After spending the night in jail, Peter and John are brought before the high priest and a council of elders to give an account of their activities, particularly the healing that Peter did for a lame man. They ask Peter, "By what power or in whose name are you doing these things?" (Acts 4:7 NIV) The Jewish leaders are trying to intimidate Peter and John. A wrong answer could land them back in jail or, even worse, dead on a cross. "Then Peter, filled with the Holy Spirit" goes on to tell them exactly in whose authority they are doing such things. But he presses his point further reminding them they rejected the Messiah. Peter isn't backing down; his days of denying his beliefs are over, and the high priests are speechless:"When they saw the courage of Peter and John and realized that they were unschooled, ordinary men, they were astonished and they took note that these men had been with Jesus. (Acts 4:13 NIV)

Peter is an unexpected Hero—a man who has struggled with the limitations of his nature. But the previous story is just one of a series of remarkable events that occur in his life, following the withdrawal of Jesus. In Chapter IV we discussed that the leaders of the early

Christian movement were the ultimate underdogs; in the words of the high priests, they were "unschooled, ordinary men." Yet somehow the movement survived in Jerusalem, and it spread throughout Judea, around the eastern rim of the Mediterranean, all the way to Rome and the far reaches of the Roman Empire.

It's a miracle the movement survived the persecution that it faced in Jerusalem alone. That it was already reshaping the Roman Empire within the lifetime of the heroic characters described in Acts is miraculous. How do we explain Peter's remarkable transformation from the man who denies Jesus in the Gospels to the man we meet throughout the Acts of the Apostles? How do we explain the conversion and work of Paul, the other prominent character in the book of Acts? How do we explain the miraculous spread of the movement and the courage of those who embraced it? The author of Acts tells us it only makes sense if we factor in another power—the indwelling work of the Holy Spirit.

Why We Need the Holy Spirit in Our Quest

There are countless ways in which the Holy Spirit might work in our own lives. In a moment I will try to bring to light how to invite the Holy Spirit into your journey. But first I want to give some specific benefits and reasons that the Holy Spirit (our SuperNatural aid) is of critical importance in our own Hero's Journey.

Wisdom and Truth

As our adventures lead us into unfamiliar territory, we will often find ourselves beyond our own comprehension and experiences. We might require perspectives we have never considered. We might need some force to illuminate the path we should travel to keep us tracking toward the final destination. The Holy Spirit conveys wisdom that the Hero may lack if he has to rely on his experiences and intellect alone. He guides us through times of darkness and uncertainty. He helps us to avoid relationships or commitments that will delay our progress and instead connect us with those that will help us. Jesus promises, "But when he, the Spirit of truth, comes, he will guide you into all the truth. He will not speak on his own; he will speak only what he hears, and he will tell you what is yet to come." (John 16:13 NIV) The Holy Spirit offers wisdom and truth.

Assurance and Love

Each quest will challenge the Hero with trials, tests and temptations. There will be times when we suffer setbacks and find ourselves discouraged or disillusioned. This is normal and should be expected, especially, if the stakes of the journey are high. Choosing to live in the field of adventure awakens the heart to feel things it hasn't felt in a long time, if ever. With the highs of an alive heart come the lows. The problem with a numb heart is that it can't be numbed selectively. When we shut our hearts off because of pain, we also shut down the ability to experience joy and hope. The Hero's Journey will often begin to melt this numbness, which will ultimately be a critical life-renewing process, but it might also bring to the surface wounds and pain that must be processed. The Spirit gives us assurance when we begin to question the wisdom of the journey or when fear threatens to thwart our progress.

The Spirit conveys the love of God and encourages us that the journey is worth it and that we have the tools at our disposal to make it through, even when we doubt it most. Jesus promises, "And I will pray to the Father, and he shall give you another Comforter, that he may be with you forever." (John 14:16 ASV) The Spirit pours out love and assurance in those bleak moments when the journey threatens to break us.

Intervention and Authority

In some cases the Spirit might intervene on our behalf. We might register this intervention or not even be aware it's happening. But a seemingly insurmountable roadblock is removed from our path and a new opportunity replaces it. A potential distraction from our quest gets addressed. A temptation that could derail us is held at bay. While the quest is not always easy, we sense that we are riding on the rhythms of destiny as our life crosses people and events that seem to be placed there by providence. The Spirit is working all along guiding us to our goal and intervening as needed to help us reach our destination. Paul writes to the church in Rome, "And he who searches our hearts knows the mind of the Spirit, because the Spirit intercedes for God's people in accordance with the will of God." (Rom. 8:27 NIV)

Making Sense of a Personal Spirit

Prior to the heroic stories told in the book of Acts, Jesus prepared his apostles for his crucifixion with a warning that he would leave them soon. Not surprisingly, they were alarmed. At one point Peter tells Jesus he is wrong and that he can't die. So Jesus tries to explain why his departure from them is required: "None of you asks me, 'Where are you going?' Rather, you are filled with grief because I have said these things. But very truly I tell you, it is for your good that I am going away. Unless I go away, the Advocate will not come to you; but if I go, I will send him to you." (John 16:6-7 NIV)

The "Advocate" whom Jesus is sending in the passage above is the Holy Spirit. This is the same Spirit Jesus received at his baptism. This same Spirit is described in the first verse of the entire Bible where it says, "The earth was formless and empty, darkness was over the surface of the deep, and the Spirit of God was hovering over the waters." (Gen 1:2 NIV) Jesus is explaining to his apostles that he will go up to heaven. The Spirit will come down, and in the terminology of the Hero's Journey, all who accept Jesus's sacrifice will receive the Spirit as their SuperNatural Aid.

In Part I of the book, we discussed that Jesus's mission was to restore humanity to its intended vocation as image-bearers of God, responsible for restoring his kingdom. Integral to that design as image-bearers is an inherent receptivity for being filled by the Spirit. The Apostle Paul wrote that "the body is a temple of the Holy Spirit." He comes to dwell inside each of us, given to us by God, to connect us with his eternal order and breathe God's holy power into our lives.

As we try to understand how the Holy Spirit might inform our own lives, I want to point out two potential stumbling blocks. First, the term "Holy Spirit" may be problematic because it can evoke a conception of God or Jesus that isn't approachable. (Some traditions call the Holy Spirit the Holy Ghost, which may be an even more challenging term.) The modern mind hears "Spirit" and is tempted to picture a formless impersonal impulse traveling like radio waves through the air or a vague mystical force operating through nature. But these impersonal conceptions miss the context of how we should understand the Holy Spirit. If we examine the way Jesus convened with the Spirit, we see that the Spirit came as his companion—a personal, relational companion. To Jesus the Spirit didn't come as an "it." The Spirit came as a friend, helper, teacher and advocate. The Spirit comes to us in the same way, not as a vague mystical force, but as a knowable, relatable character.

Some Christian groups will try to skirt this problematic terminology of "Spirit" by admonishing followers to engage in a personal relationship with Jesus Christ and learn a lot about him. They focus on the character of Jesus and how much he loved us to die on a Cross. They explore the timeless wisdom of his teachings. While this is productive work, it raises a second problem: how do we have a personal relationship with someone who died 2,000 year ago?

We have no other examples of having a "relationship" with a historical figure. For example, my literary hero is C. S. Lewis. I have read almost everything he wrote, and he has played an important role in my spiritual formation. But I don't have a relationship with C. S. Lewis. A relationship requires an ongoing interaction with another person in which intangible emotions such as love are expressed and shared within a dynamic exchange. I know a lot about C. S. Lewis, but I will never know him. Is reading about Jesus's life and studying the parables he told sufficient for having a "personal" relationship with him? Is knowing about Jesus the same as knowing Jesus? While studying his life and teachings shouldn't be discounted, he and the Spirit offer far more.

In Christian theological terms, the Holy Spirit is one member of the Trinity, which is the doctrine of one God who eternally exists as three distinct persons—the Father, the Son (Jesus) and the Holy Spirit. Each person of the Trinity is fully God, working in a perfect loving, eternal relationship with the others. Each member has a role to play in creation. In this relationship "the central role of the Spirit is to reveal Christ and to unite us to him and to all those who participate in his body. Just as the indwelling of Christ and the indwelling of the Spirit are two aspects of one and the same reality in the New Testament, so to sustain us 'in Christ' is the heart and soul of the Spirit's ministry"[1]

In other words, it's the Spirit who manifests Jesus to each of us, which allows Jesus to be our personal guide 2,000 years after his death. Jesus's love is perceived and his personality is revealed through the Spirit. Starting with those Heroes we read about in the book of Acts all the way until the present, it's the Holy Spirit who makes the personal presence of Jesus known to all who seek him.

The Apostle Paul wrote, "The first man Adam became a living being; the last Adam, a life-giving spirit." (1 Cor 15:45) Jesus is the last Adam, and with his death, resurrection and ascension, he becomes one with the Spirit, his intimate ally throughout his life, and he returns to us in coordination with the Spirit. "As a result, when he [the Holy Spirit] comes to Christians to indwell them, he comes as the Spirit of Christ in such a way that to possess him is to possess Christ himself, just as to lack him is to lack Christ."[2] The Spirit and Jesus, though distinct, are inseparable. Even Paul hints at this in his writings, sometimes using the terms "Jesus," "Spirit" and "Spirit of Jesus" interchangeably, as if they all implied the same effect on the recipient.

At this point my intent is not to venture into the theological complexities and intricacies of the Trinity. What I am hoping to highlight is that the indwelling of the Spirit provides the recipient with a path to experience God's presence, reflected by the personality of Jesus. What does this mean for our purposes here? It means that God is offering us a deep, soulful and intimate friendship. He speaks to our hearts personally. And he is interested, even delighted, in each of us. Furthermore, through the Spirit, God transforms us into the likeness of Jesus, directs our paths, provides us with encouragement and breathes into our own earthly activities and relationships his life-giving force.

Connecting to the Holy Spirit

While discernment of the Holy Spirit is a practiced skill that results in greater awareness over time, any one of us may enter into a personal relationship with Jesus through the gift of the Holy Spirit. This isn't a relationship reserved for professional clergy. Nor do we have to wait until we have our acts cleaned up to begin. Jesus is waiting for all of us who seek him, regardless of our current moral conditions or position on earth. Each of us, by the Holy Spirit, have been adopted into God's family, and we are no longer slaves to our former limits. We are heirs with Jesus.

The first step in accepting SuperNatural aid is to make the leap discussed in Chapter III, submitting to the posture required to move from the head to the heart and to experience the reality of God that goes beyond the intellect and sufficiency of words. The theological explanations of the work of the Holy Spirit and a triune God may conceptualize God's vital activity to the intellect, but to experience this vitality in our lives, we must embrace faith. Over the centuries millions upon millions of people have testified to the indwelling work of the Holy Spirit, including his powers, mysteries and revelations. To begin is a choice: we can ignore our SuperNatural aid or surrender to the deep mystery of the Holy Spirit and simply invite him to join us even though we may not yet know what that means or how it works.

Once we have affirmed this possibility of having Jesus take an active role in our life through the work of the Holy Spirit, the next step is to invite him to reveal his personal presence and character to us. We might begin by reading the Bible, knowing as we move into a deeper relationship that the inspiration we find from the Spirit will not contradict the timeless truths memorialized in the contents of scripture.

The next step is to seek times of quiet stillness during which we can open our hearts to the possibility that the Spirit will speak to us personally. In those times of "listening," we might become attuned to the impressions he leaves in our innermost being. Words, images and subtle promptings might arise from deep inside, but at the same time they may feel as though they come from somewhere or someone else.

These inspirations are just enough out of place from our own typical thought processes and conventional inner monologues to bring awareness to the possibility of an inspired source.

These heart impressions usually come in times of deep reflection. This is especially true when we have an unpracticed ear for such discernment. "Hearing" or "sensing" the words and inspirations of the Spirit in our Hearts is difficult to impossible if we never have time to quiet the incessant buzzing of the world and settle into regular uninterrupted times for listening and receiving. Prayers of petition, in which we half-heartedly ask God to perform miracles or protect us from something are not the only way to connect with Jesus and bring his power to bear in the world. "Listening" is perhaps an even more important skill in prayer. If prayer is something you do, but most of the time you just list requests, you might begin spending more time asking questions and then listening to the movements of that still quiet voice.

Describing how to discern the Spirit's movements to someone else is difficult. For one thing, it's a very personal experience. For example, my wife and I can look at each other in certain situations and know exactly what the other is thinking. But if I had to describe to someone else how to read those cues from her, I don't think I could, in part because I would have to describe more than just the nonverbal cues. It's a "sense" based on our shared history and the spirit of our relationship. I think the Spirit of Jesus is personal like that with us, too. The other reason it would be difficult to describe is that we are in territory that goes beyond common sensory explanations and requires intuition that can't be learned except through real-world experience.

So, with the caveat on the limitations of any written manual on what it means to convene with Jesus through the Spirit, let me offer a few more potential starting points. We might try becoming more attuned to the stirring in our hearts. Sometimes the Spirit might awaken deep desires and longings that light us up and make us feel alive. God promises in the scriptures "I will give them a heart to know Me, for I am the LORD; and they will be My people, and I will be their God, for they will return to Me with their whole heart." (Jer. 24:7 NIV) Our hearts, the seat of our will, desire and creative imagination—the truest unfiltered part of our unique identities—has been restored by the Spirit of Jesus and equipped to know him and be with him relationally. We should not ignore those moments of awe, inspiration and gratitude that sometimes surprise us and attach themselves to a bigger purpose for our lives.

The Spirit sometimes uses the counsel of others to help us on our journey. Words spoken to us may direct our attention toward the truth. Perhaps the Spirit is preparing us, and our directive becomes clear when a mentor or a close friend offers a perspective we couldn't see on our own. Sometimes the Spirit works through our relationships, not only to offer advice and perspective, but also to provide encouragement, love and assistance.

Words of wisdom may also come in the form of lyrics in a song or perhaps a paragraph written by a favorite author. The Spirit might stir us through nature herself. These words, lyrics and interactions with nature have a different tenor, allowing them to break through our normal field of experience, awakening our heart to an awareness of deeper truths. For example, we might have listened to the same song a hundred times and never noticed the line from the song that now, suddenly brings tears to our eyes and a lump to our throats. That internal shift and surprising emotional response could be the Spirit of Jesus working within us.

The Spirit might manifest himself through our circumstances and serendipitous timing of events in our life to draw our attention to his activity. Jung's term for this was "synchronicity," the strange coincidences in life that come together to direct our paths and to bring our awareness to the grand narrative unfolding throughout creation. The Spirit helps us find our place in the larger story.

Learning to abide in the Spirit and to discern his movement in our life is a process of maturation. The Hero learns with each journey how to better work alongside his SuperNatural aid. As the Hero grows, so will his intimacy with the Spirit, and the Hero becomes more attuned to the Spirit's "voice," enabling the Hero to respond more decisively to the Spirit's instruction. We can only learn to listen by trying and seeing what happens: taking a risk, listening and following. We may be surprised how God starts showing up.

Lastly, Notable twentieth-century theologian, Hans Urs von Balthasar, wrote, "Lovers are the ones who know most about God; the theologian must listen to them."[3] God's clearest revelation comes in the form of love. His example for us is the crucifixion, and through the Holy Spirit, he makes the purity and otherworldliness of his love apparent to each individual believer. No explanation will ever come close to what is communicated through his love. Nor will the Spirit come to condemn and criticize. Those voices we hear that tell us all about the bad parts of ourselves and make us feel ashamed are not from God, for we are told that there is now "no condemnation for those in Christ." We become a new creation and as the Holy Spirit lays bare what is meant by this love, he transforms us, the believers, into something more than bystanders. We become active participants in this divine love, and our life takes on the dimension of the greatest Hero's life. We are Heroes because Jesus was a Hero, and he is working alongside us to make our life reflect his life.

CHAPTER IX

ROAD OF TRIALS

Crossing the First Threshold

After committing to the call and gaining the assurances of the SuperNatural aid, the Hero must officially cross into the field of adventure. Very often he immediately comes upon the first guardian barring his way forward. The guardian stands between the Hero and an unknown realm full of danger and uncertainty. To deal with the guardian of the First Threshold is risky business. This is no benevolent force that stands at the outer limit of the Hero's current sphere of power and understanding. To continue his journey, the Hero must deal with the guardian and sneak past him into the greater unknown.

IN GREEK MYTHOLOGY a three-headed dog named Cerberus blocks the path to the underworld. Any Hero who wants to retrieve something from that mysterious land must navigate his way past the giant canine. In *Star Wars* Luke's Threshold Guardian is his uncle, reminding Luke of his duties and obligations at home. When Luke is finally ready to head off on his own adventure his uncle tells him, "You can't leave. I need you for one more harvest." If the Hero wants to go on his adventure, he has to find a way past the Threshold Guardian. This is an initial test of the Hero's commitment. If the Hero can't get past the guardian, he probably isn't ready for all that the journey will ask of him. Becoming a Hero isn't easy. If everyone could do it, then we wouldn't bother telling stories about them. Only those who are worthy are allowed to pass into the "special world" of the story, and it's the job of the Threshold Guardian to weed out those who are not ready.

In everyday life a person might be the Threshold Guardian, but the Threshold Guardian could also come in the form of a circumstantial or psychological obstacle. As we gain assurance that we are ready to cross the First Threshold into the mysterious world beyond, the Threshold Guardian sounds the alarm bell and raises the stakes to remind us what we could lose or to tell us the journey is foolish. The motive of the Threshold Guardian is not necessarily malicious. Sometimes the Threshold Guardian believes he is protecting us by keeping us out of harm's way.

For example, a parent can often be a Threshold Guardian in both stories and in real life. The parent might be the stereotypically overprotective kind, fearing the uncertainty of the son or daughter venturing beyond the parent's own comfort zone. Sometimes the Threshold Guardian is the carefully laid path in life planned for the

Hero by his family. The family has expectations about what type of careers are acceptable, what kind of spouse is suitable and what type of hobbies are worthy of pursuit. But the Hero must discover his own path through life. Even late into adulthood, parents might intervene or interject their opinions to keep the Hero on the path that the parents have dreamed up. When the Hero wants to answer the Call to Adventure, the parents' objections raise the stakes of the quest and test the resolve of the would-be Hero. This blocking of the way by the parents could also take the form of shielding the would-be Hero from hardships and stepping in to save the day whenever he encounters difficulties instead of allowing him to navigate through life's difficulties on his own. This doesn't just happen with children or teenagers. The "helicopter parents" of today might try to bar the child's way into the field of adventure well into adulthood.

Other personifications of the Threshold Guardians could be a risk-averse boss or a peer group that doesn't understand or appreciate the journey. A religious leader can sometimes play the role of the Threshold Guardian. Perhaps the leader doesn't want to lose influence and fears what the Hero might discover beyond the religious leader's own comfort zone. The Threshold Guardian could come in the form of current life circumstances, such as the balance in the would-be Hero's checking account. The would-be Hero wants to take a risk and cross the threshold but is frozen by the potential financial risk. Or the Threshold Guardian could represent something psychological. Maybe the would-be Hero has been hurt when he has taken risks in the past. He doesn't believe in himself or doubts whether he deserves what he is dreaming of finding at the end of the journey.

If the Hero makes it past the Threshold and sneaks past the Guardian, there is no turning back. This is the point in life where the Hero stops talking about his dreams and begins living them. You may have made up your mind many times that you were ready for the adventure, but when you got to the point where you had to make the commitment real the Threshold Guardian backed you down. When you are ready to fight your way past, then you are ready to enter the Initiation phase of the Hero's Journey.

Road of Trials

As the Hero learns to take mastery over his new powers and the rules of this new world, he faces a perilous path of challenges. The ordeals he faces during this phase are a deepening of the problems he faced in crossing the first threshold. The dangers have not subsided, and the questions about the Hero's character and future destiny remain unanswered. Many times these trials will come in sets of three, and the Hero may at times stumble and even fail. There will also be momentary victories and glimpses of a world and existence as it was meant to be before the conflict continues.

After Crossing the Threshold marked by the Jordan River, Jesus spends forty days in the desert where the Devil tests him three times. The first test comes in the form of economic temptation. The Devil knows Jesus has gone without food for many days, so he comes to him and says, "You must be hungry! If you are the Son of God, then why don't you turn these stones to bread?" But Jesus passes the first test, replying "It is written; that man shall not live on bread alone." The Devil moves on to his next test for Jesus, presenting him with a political temptation. He takes Jesus to the top of a mountain and in an instant shows Jesus all of the kingdoms of the world. The Devil says to him, "You can have authority over all this and all of the people will bow to you, if you will worship me." Jesus refuses saying, "It is written; Worship the Lord your God and serve him only." The last of the three tests in the wilderness comes in the form of spiritual temptation. The Devil leads Jesus up to the top of the highest point of the Temple and says, "If you are so spiritual, then throw yourself off." Then quoting scripture, the Devil says, "Surely God will bear you up and you won't be harmed." Again, Jesus refuses the Devil's overtures replying, "Do not put the Lord your God to the test." Then the scriptures say that the Devil leaves Jesus "until a more opportune time." The Devil is not finished with his harassment, but Jesus has triumphed in this first set of tests. He is ready to take on his next challenge.[1]

Even after Jesus completes his test in the wilderness, he still faces other trials until his culminating ordeal on the Cross. Throughout his ministry the Jewish religious leaders plot against him. On multiple occasions they try to entrap him, trick him or have him arrested. In one exchange the Pharisees come and ask Jesus in front of a crowd, "Is it right to pay the imperial tax or not?" (Matt 22:17) Jesus knows what they are trying to do, and he asks in return, "Why are you trying to trap me?" (Matt 22:18) The Pharisees' question is designed to get Jesus in trouble with someone. Whichever side he chooses, he loses. If he says the people should not pay the imperial tax, this could land him in trouble with the Roman authorities. On the other hand, the Jews resent the rule of a foreign government and despise the onerous taxes imposed on them by Rome. To them only God is sovereign, and paying taxes to a Gentile ruler is an abomination. Jesus wisely tells the crowd, "Give back to Caesar what is Caesar's and to God what is God's." (Matt 22:21) And the crowd was amazed by his answer.

The Road of Trials characterizes the part of the journey before the decisive turning point of the story. There will be a final exam the Hero must pass. The trials along the way serve as the quizzes and tests the Hero must navigate in preparation for the final exam. The trials may delay, frighten or, in some unfortunate cases, thwart the Hero's Journey altogether. But the Hero who passes the quizzes and tests successfully gains the skills and confidence that he needs to complete the journey ahead.

Enemies

In *The Wizard of Oz*, Dorothy encounters a series of trials along the Yellow Brick Road. She learns that her enemy, the Wicked Witch, shadows her every turn and is bent on destroying Dorothy before she reaches Oz. The Wicked Witch enchants an orchard of angry apple trees to become Dorothy's enemies. In another scene she hurls a fireball at Dorothy and her friends. As Dorothy and her traveling companions get near the City of Oz, the Wicked Witch puts a field of poppies in their path, sending Dorothy into an opium-induced sleep.

Although the road to Oz is full of wonderful surprises and new friends, it's a difficult road to travel. The Road of Trials has an essential purpose for Dorothy, as it does for every Hero. By the time Dorothy reaches the final Atoning Act, she has learned a great deal about herself and the ways of the mysterious world of Oz. Her resolve has been tested, and she has grown wise to the ways in which her enemies operate.

We might face a variety of enemies on our journey who will work on us through our fears and feelings of inadequacy. These enemies could be real people in our path who want us to fail or want to protect the status quo that we seek to change. These enemies could be psychological scars in us that create doubt or bring up memories of past pain. The enemies could be spiritual, beyond our common sensory awareness but real nonetheless. Jesus warns us, "The thief comes only to steal and kill and destroy." (John 10:10 NIV) He is referring to an enemy that stalks us from the spiritual realm but is real nonetheless.

The outcome of the Hero's Journey includes greater freedom to live according to our intended purposes and bringing the gifts of that freedom to the people in our lives. But that kind of objective does not go unopposed. Sometimes it will be obvious when our enemies are operating on the Road to Trials. We see them standing in our way, hurling fireballs in our direction. At other times the opposition comes more subtly, drawing us off the path unknowingly until we find ourselves lost and ensnared. Regardless of whether the opposition is in the form of a frontal attack or guerrilla warfare, we would do well to expect it and to factor in that we won't go skipping down the Yellow Brick Road without being harassed. Not everyone wants us to succeed, and some enemies fear what might happen if we prevail in our quest.

Temptations

As the Hero masters his newfound powers, he might be tempted, as Jesus was by the Devil, to use his position, power and knowledge for other purposes than those required to fulfill his mission. In *The Lord of the Rings*, Frodo carries a ring of frightening power. He has been marked for the mission because he is the only one who has the moral and emotional makeup to carry the ring without giving into the irresistible temptation it offers. Even some of Frodo's allies will lose their heads and try to take the ring; its allure is almost unimaginable.

In carrying the temptation of the ring around his neck, Frodo bears a tremendous burden. On his journey he is constantly tempted to use the ring's power, but Frodo understands that, if he gives in, it will be the end of him, the end of his journey and the end of Middle-earth.

We may face great temptations on our journey that are designed to lure, attract and seduce us into doing something we shouldn't be doing. They create a dilemma; is this worth giving up my quest for? An inappropriate relationship develops, or an old habit resurfaces. Giving in to the temptation once leads to giving again and again until we have created a new false adventure altogether that will lead us toward heartbreak and ruin. Or maybe our journey is going well, and we get positive recognition for all we are accomplishing. The adulation from others can go to one's head. The temptation of pride creeps in, our motives change and with them the mission's aim changes too, becoming all about our own advancement and promotion instead of the greater purpose that we set out to accomplish from the beginning.

Spiritual pride may be particularly insidious and a tremendous temptation for those who have made religion or spirituality an important part of their lives. In the third temptation of Jesus, the Devil wanted Jesus to think to himself, "I am so spiritually superior to the flesh and this earth, I will show you how great I am." As God incarnate Jesus could have rightfully puffed himself up spiritually, but that would have defeated the purpose of his mission, which was to experience the limitations of the flesh so that he could rescue the rest of humanity from it. As we travel the Hero's path, we may experience moments of enlightenment or insight that others have not benefited from, and we may be tempted to think of ourselves as wise and in possession of special knowledge. As spiritual pride sets in, the Hero becomes closed to new experiences and perspectives, believing he knows the only way. The focus shifts from helping others to proving that he and his methods are better than others and their methods. He loses the humility required for honest self-examination and spiritual pride derails the mission.

Training

Sometimes the Road of Trials begins in the care of a mentor who challenges the Hero and trains him in the ways of the new world the Hero has just discovered. The mentor knows what is required for the Hero to make it through the journey and, through special and sometimes difficult training, prepares him for the greater enemies and temptations to come. The mentor may put the Hero through certain tests by which he learns important lessons about himself and how to harness his own powers for good. He may find this work exhausting, frustrating and pointless to begin with and may want to give up the training before he has gained the perspective on how it will benefit him.

In *Star Wars*, Obi-wan-Kenobi trains Luke about the Force and how to use the weapon of the Jedi, the lightsaber. In the movie the *Matrix*, Neo trains with Morpheus in various training simulations before going out to face the agents bent on destroying him. In the *Karate Kid*, Miyagi makes Daniel perform hours of manual labor around Miyagi's house until Daniel becomes indignant and threatens to quit. He wants to learn karate, not wax Miyagi's cars and paint his fence. Miyagi finally shows Daniel how the movements of all the manual work Daniel has done have preconditioned him with important karate defense techniques.

We all need mentors on our journeys—people who can see beyond what we can see and have already walked a similar path to the one we seek. Effective mentors will challenge us and may even seem at times like they are making the road more difficult. The mentors we should seek aren't people who only offer encouragement, although that is certainly important, but who also challenge us to grow, ask us hard questions and suggest solutions that don't always seem the most expedient or easy ones. They hold us accountable to our own commitments and help us find clarity when the limitations of our own maturity and experience cloud our thinking.

The Interesting Case of Visionaries

Have you noticed that nearly all of the famous visionaries faced significant hardship, rejection and failure on their way to success? Thomas Edison invented the lightbulb but not without making over 10,000 unsuccessful attempts first. When asked why he didn't give up after 9,000 attempts, he replied, "Why would I feel like a failure? And why would I ever give up? I now know definitely over 9,000 ways an electric lightbulb will not work. Success is almost in my grasp."[2] Edison also founded the iconic American company, General Electric, and when he died had over 1,000 patents to his name. Despite this tremendous success, Edison's teachers had told him growing up that he was too stupid to learn anything. When he joined the workforce, he was fired from his first two jobs for not being "productive enough."

J. K. Rowling started writing the first *Harry Potter* book in 1990 but experienced a series of personal setbacks along the way. Her mother died shortly after she began writing. Rowling went through a divorce while living in a foreign country. She battled depression and at one point was so penniless that she had to go on government welfare. By 1993, three years after beginning to write *Harry Potter*, she had only three chapters written. She finally finished writing the book in 1995, but the manuscript was rejected by all of the major publishers in England. The book was eventually picked up by a small publisher in 1997. Rowling received a paltry £1,500 advance, and only a thousand copies of *Harry Potter* were initially published (with half being sent to public libraries).[3] We know Rowling as the prolific author who has sold over 400 million books, but her path to success was difficult and uncertain.

After Walt Disney's first company, Laugh-O-gram Films, went bankrupt, he picked up and moved from Kansas City to California with forty dollars in his pocket. His second animation company didn't go bankrupt but was essentially stolen because he hadn't taken the legal measures to protect his ownership of the characters his company was creating. On his third try, Walt conceived of a cartoon mouse, which would become the symbol of the company that bears his name to this day. But the early years of the Walt Disney Company were anything but easy. At one point Walt suffered a nervous breakdown from the stress of running the business. He ran up against artist's strikes, which threatened the company's survival. After the United States entered World War II in 1941, the U.S. Army took over the Walt Disney Studio and turned it into a tank repair shop. The disruption of war almost bankrupted the company, and it struggled to repay its large debts.[4]

Disney's dream to build a theme park for kids also came with great opposition and setbacks. Every lender turned him down until he convinced a new television network called ABC to finance the theme park in exchange for Disney providing them content. But even the park's opening was a near disaster. Today we know Walt Disney as the visionary behind the premier media and entertainment companies in the world, and his parks have been called "The Happiest Place on Earth" for generations of visitors. But Disney wasn't viewed as a visionary by his contemporaries. His eccentric and far-fetched vision of the future didn't make sense until after he was successful.

These stories are not exceptions. Many of the most revered people from history, business and politics faced tremendous trials on their way to becoming successful and winning our admiration. In an interview with journalist Bill Moyers, Joseph Campbell offered an interesting perspective on why the path of the visionary is often so challenging— why to onlookers the visionary sometimes seems on the edge of neuroticism:

> *They've moved out of the society that would have protected them, and into the dark forest, into the world of fire, of original experience. Original experience has not been interpreted for you, and so you've got to work out your life for yourself. Either you can take it or you can't. You don't have to go far off the inter- preted path to find yourself in very difficult situations. The courage to face the trials and to bring a whole new body of pos- sibilities into the field of interpreted experience for other people to experience—that is the hero's deed.[5]*

Not every Hero's quest will end with a famous invention, book, company or other feat remembered in history books. The point is that throughout our lives, most of us rely on the scripts that other people or society have provided for us to determine how we should act. We don't know who we are, and so we rely on others to interpret our life for us. The Hero, on the other hand, ventures into new territory and new experiences. Instead of working out the rules of the game for him and telling him where he should seek life, the Hero sees the world through a different lens. He is not a copycat or a conformist. In this sense he is a visionary, seeing the world not as it is, but as it should be.

Desirable Difficulties

In his book, *David and Goliath*, best-selling author Malcolm Gladwell outlines a startling and unexpected discovery in his research that he labels the "Theory of Desirable Difficulties." Gladwell asserts that sometimes things that are viewed as difficulties in one part of a person's life lead to advantages in another part of that person's life. Gladwell uses the example of dyslexia—a challenging learning disorder that makes reading extremely difficult—to support his theory:

> *Can dyslexia turn out to be a desirable difficulty? It is hard to believe that it can, given how many people struggle with the disorder throughout their lives— except for a strange fact. An extraordinarily high number of successful entrepreneurs are dyslexic. A recent study by Julie Logan at City University London puts the number somewhere around a third. The list includes many of the most famous innovators of the past few decades. Richard Branson, the British billionaire entrepreneur, is dyslexic. Charles Schwab, the founder of the discount brokerage that bears his name, is dyslexic, as are the cell phone pioneer Craig McCaw; David Neeleman, the founder of JetBlue; John Chambers, the CEO of the technology giant Cisco; Paul Orfalea, the founder of Kinko's— to name just a few. The neuroscientist Sharon Thompson-Schill remembers speaking at a meeting of prominent university donors— virtually all of them successful business people— and on a whim asking how many of them had ever been diagnosed with a learning disorder. "Half the hands went up," she said. "It was unbelievable."* [6]

In many cases the people studied grew up in a time when dyslexia wasn't even diagnosed, so they struggled terribly in school. They were told they were dumb, lazy or both and were subject to tremendous frustration growing up. How could this possibly be an advantage? Gladwell explains that, because they have great difficulty reading, children with dyslexia are forced to develop other strategies that prove useful later in their lives. They are forced to find a new path through life because the path their peers are traveling and the path that society expects them to travel don't work for them. In the context of the Road of Trials, what Gladwell is suggesting is that these disadvantages meant that people with dyslexia cannot rely on interpreted experience and the paths laid out for their peers—those paths don't work or are far too painful for people with dyslexia. They have to find their own way and create their own experience, which has some inherent advantages when they enter the workforce. There was no other choice for them but to move out from the society that should have protected them and work out their life for themselves. In the process they discover and hone traits that they might not have discovered otherwise.

Of course, nobody would wish a difficulty such as dyslexia on a child. Gladwell points out that there is a diminishing return to difficulties. Too many difficulties can crush a person. It's one thing to have dyslexia and come from an upper-middle-class family with a cohesive and supportive home life; it's quite another to have dyslexia and come from a broken home in a poor neighborhood. The point is that setbacks, difficulties and trials are not signs that our own journey is heading in the wrong direction. They very well might signal the opposite, so that with each hurdle we overcome, we are better prepared for the larger tests ahead. The trials often signal that we have moved beyond the story everyone else expects us to tell with our lives and toward our own authentic story. None of us desires difficulties in our life, but sometimes what we see as difficulties or "disorders" are only difficulties because they make it challenging to live in the status quo and conventional. When we realize that we were meant to be original, we can begin to understand how some difficulties might be to our advantage in the long run.

The Big and Little Trials We Face

Anytime we move outside the conventions of our old way of life, we may experience friction with those institutions and conventions that have supported and defined us. And those frictions create their own set of trials to test our convictions and challenge us to grow.

For example, our quest may transform us in a way our family of origin (parents, siblings) don't understand. They may be used to a certain dynamic in our relationship with them; the grooves of the family's way of relating are well worn and, although there may be a high level of dysfunction, everyone has gotten comfortable with it. We begin to grow, and the old grooves of relating don't work anymore. While we aren't trying to be adversarial, our family is not sure how to relate to the new person we are becoming. They aren't sure they are comfortable with our new approach to life and relationships. They may misinterpret our motives, and so conflict arises.

The same scenario can play out in other relationships or groups that we are a part of. Our job, church, community activities and so on all have an unwritten spirit that governs the way everyone interacts. We have learned to play a role, but as we take the Hero's journey, we experience these different parts of our life with an original lens. When we begin to change, it can upset the comfortable unspoken dynamics. Some people will cheer us, glad we have the courage to step up, speak up and do something. Others will not approve and will work to neutralize the threat we pose by opposing our path forward. They may confront us or gossip about us. They may leave us out of important decisions. Sometimes the people who oppose us may not even realize they are undermining us. They may not even be able to name why our convictions and authenticity unnerves them.

In his book *Wild at Heart*, John Eldredge advises, "Let people feel the weight of who you are and let them deal with it."[7] As we travel the Hero's Journey and change, our relationships change as well. This isn't an invitation to be insensitive to others—hopefully, the opposite is the case. But as we succeed in our journey, we come to realize that the best gift we can give the world is our truest self. We don't have to pretend to be someone others want us to be. As we write our true story, we hope that everyone will line up to applaud our endeavors, especially those closest to us, but many won't understand or feel comfortable dealing with the weight of who we are. That's fine. Let them deal with it.

Allies

In all great stories, the Hero rallies his allies around his mission. Jesus gathered his twelve disciples. Frodo had the fellowship of the ring, a diverse crew of warriors to help him navigate the dangerous landscape of Middle-earth. Dorothy had the Scarecrow, Tinman, and Lion as she wandered the Yellow Brick Road. Allies have similar objectives, and they help share the burden of the journey. They fight alongside the Hero, rescue the Hero and summon the SuperNatural aid on behalf of the Hero.

We need allies in our journey as well, people in our life who know us authentically, our backstory, our weaknesses, our fears and our desires. We need allies we can turn to for help when the Road of Trials gets difficult. I know in my life how important authentic community has been, and I am not sure how anyone can thrive in this world without it. There is a strong tendency for us to isolate ourselves when life gets tough. For some reason, disappointments and failures make us feel alone, and often it's when we need others the most that we feel least like engaging with them. We don't want to be a burden on our friends, or we fear that if they knew we were struggling so much with a certain issue, they wouldn't feel the same way about us.

There is a powerful scene in *The Lord of the Rings* in which Frodo tries to continue his trip toward Mordor alone. He doesn't know if he can trust his allies any longer because the power of the ring he carries is threatening to tear apart the friends who are accompanying him. Frodo finds a small boat, and as he paddles away alone across the river, his best friend, Sam, plunges into the water after him. Frodo screams at Sam to go back because Sam can't swim. Frodo has to stop and pull Sam out of the water to save him from drowning. When Sam is safely in the boat, he tells Frodo, "I made a promise, a promise. 'Don't you leave him 'Samwise Gangie,' And I don't mean to." Sam won't let Frodo take the journey alone. He will risk his life for his friend, and he will end up literally walking through the pits of hell to support Frodo in his quest. We all need allies like that.

This is a critical step if we are going to take the Hero's Journey. We must identify our allies and make a commitment to each other to be as real and as raw as imaginable. We need someone or a group of people in a similar phase of life as us and who share similar desires about the type of life they want to lead. We need to cultivate those relationships. We need to take risks and pour ourselves out like Sam did for Frodo. We shouldn't travel the Road of Trials alone when we don't have to. We should share the burden and the joys of the adventure with people we can call "brother" or "sister."

Finding Our Purpose

As we contemplate whether it's worth answering our next Call to Adventure, we should understand that life will bring us trials no matter what. Whether we embark on the Hero's Journey or not, we all face challenges and setbacks. Most people just endure the trials in their life, become numb and try their best to survive. They don't have a purpose, so they float through life without direction, just responding the best they know how in the moment. The Hero's Journey may bring its own trials and temptations but with a critical difference—the trials the Hero faces are tied to a larger story and a greater purpose. We don't have to navigate the difficulties in our path or overcome our shortcomings and then wonder what the point of it all was. We are in constant training for the decisive turning points of life still to come, and trials are fertile training ground. Weaknesses may turn into strengths. Old perspectives may turn into a new awareness about our life and the world.

CHAPTER X

ATONEMENT WITH THE FATHER

In this phase the Hero must confront the thing that holds the ultimate power over his life, usually represented by the Father. This is also a step of initiation, and if the Hero is properly prepared, he becomes like the Father (AT-ONE-MENT), but if he is initiated before he is ready, he won't be able to handle the powers that come with the Atonement. In many cases before the Hero can move in the direction of the Father, he must first learn to see the Father in the light of his mercy and grace. This is part of the growth process of the Hero as he comes to understand the inaccuracies of his infantile views of the Father as only a mercurial and vengeful force. As he endures the crisis and terror that are apt to come as part of the Atonement, he sees the truth about the Father. The world of crisis melts away into the life-breathing perpetual manifestation of the Father's presence.

WE HAVE REACHED THE CENTRAL CRISIS of the Hero's Journey. The Atonement phase is also called the "Supreme Ordeal." It's the most important trial the Hero must endure. This is the part of the story in which the Hero dies in some real or symbolic way to be reborn into a new and better way of life. This is the key dramatic element of every story: a relationship ends, an enterprise fails, an old personality trait dies, a great fear is confronted. The Hero who survives or is reborn after the Supreme Ordeal, has accomplished the most important part of his quest. He has tasted death and no longer lives in fear.

While the Supreme Ordeal may be brought about through external circumstances, it is the point in the journey when the Hero must travel inward. The dragon that the Hero must slay is the dragon living inside him, guarding his imprisoned heart. Through the external events of the Hero's story a more important challenge is activated within. In storytelling the most common Supreme Ordeal is a showdown between the Hero and a dark opposing force—a villain, a shadowy figure, an opponent or nature herself must be overcome. But what these opponents often symbolize in the story are the Hero's negative possibilities, his own weaknesses and character defects. In other words, the Hero's greatest adversary is often himself. The struggle initiated by the antagonist serves as a kind of blessing in disguise. The resistance forces the Hero to respond and deal as necessary with the negative forces within. Without the struggle, he might be tempted to sneak past the central part of his story without facing the things in his life that have the ultimate power over him.

In *Star Wars* Luke must confront Darth Vader, whom he discovers is his father. Darth Vader embodies the results of living from the dark side of the Force. How Luke handles this encounter will determine the galaxy's future. Will he give in to fear and anger as his father did or choose a path of love and forgiveness?

In *The Wizard of Oz*, Dorothy faces her Supreme Ordeal when the Wicked Witch imprisons her and her friends in the Wicked Witch's castle. The Wicked Witch tells Dorothy that she will have to watch as the she kills each of Dorothy's friends and begins by lighting the Scarecrow on fire. Dorothy, responding out of instinct, picks up a bucket of water, and in trying to douse the fire, also splashes the water on the Wicked Witch, melting her in the process. Dorothy, without realizing that the water would kill the Witch, has not only saved the Scarecrow but also destroyed her enemy. The Land of Oz and its various characters in the movie symbolize an internal struggle that Dorothy is trying to confront. Dorothy's backstory is that both of her parents have died, leaving Dorothy feeling alone, disconnected and incomplete. Her journey through Oz is about the completion and maturing of her personality so that she can find her "home" again in the world. The Wicked Witch symbolizes the world and the parts of Dorothy's personality that keep her separated and lost. Until the Wicked Witch dies, she will always threaten and thwart the completion of Dorothy's journey to return "home."

Joseph Campbell pointed out that throughout mythology it's the Father who most often holds the ultimate power over the Hero's life. The Hero somehow becomes separated from the Father's love and protection. This doesn't necessarily happen because of what the Father has done but often because of the Hero's misinterpretation of the Father's intentions. The goal of the Atonement (or Supreme Ordeal) is reconciliation with the Father so that the Hero can come to live under the Father's love. Labeling this phase of the story the Atonement refers to its intended outcome: AT-ONE-MENT with the Father.

Campbell believed that the Atonement phase signified the death of the ego, which is the goal of the Hero's Journey: to move beyond the old limited vision of things into a state of greater consciousness and connectedness. In mythology the Father is the symbolic manifestation of deep psychological constraints, the parts of our self-conception built around the lies we believe about ourselves, the Father and the world we inhabit.

The role of the Father is to bestow identity upon his children. So, if we misinterpret his intent, we misconstrue vital assumptions as we form our own self-conceptions. We place arbitrary limits on our views of ourselves, cutting us off from our authentic self and the realization of our full potential. The way to move beyond these self-imposed constraints is to face the terror of those fears that have defined us. When we have endured them successfully, we find that they no longer have the same power over us. We see them with a new perspective, and if those fears are symbolically represented by the Father, we see him differently, too. We see the truth about ourselves and our relationship to the Father—we live in AT-ONE-MENT with him. We transcend the old boundaries of our selfhood. Past hurts and weaknesses become sources of joy and glory brought to the world to help others in their journeys.

Jesus's Atonement

On the night before Jesus's Supreme Ordeal on the Cross, he goes to the Garden of Gethsemane and stays awake throughout the night praying and agonizing over the hours to come. He tells his friends, "My soul is overwhelmed with sorrow to the point of death." (Matt 26:38 NIV) Three different times he goes and prays to God, "My Father, if it is possible, may this cup be taken from me. Yet not as I will, but as you will." (Matt 26:39) His act of Atonement will require the greatest of all sacrifices; torture, humiliation and death await him. In the end he will have a moment of feeling completely abandoned by the Father. During Jesus's anguished wait, God, the Father, does not change the mission for Jesus. Jesus must bear his cup. The Father knows death will not be the end of this story. Instead, the concluding act will be marked by a rebirth demonstrating all of the Father's power and glory to the world with Jesus, the son, sharing fully in it.

In Christian circles Atonement is often associated with punishment. Certainly, the Cross has something to do with suffering and Christ paying a penalty, but to think Atonement equals punishment is misleading. First, neither Jesus nor any of the New Testament writers use the word *Atonement*. It's a term thought up later by religious people. The central theme of Jesus's Atonement focuses on reconciliation and unification. This can't be understated when we look to what Jesus accomplished. The Atonement is about Jesus and the Father becoming one, and then through the work of the Spirit, becoming one with those created in the Father's image. Paul summarizes this mystical transformation:

> *Therefore, if anyone is in Christ, the new creation has come: The old has gone, the new is here! All this is from God, who reconciled us to himself through Christ and gave us the ministry of reconciliation: that God was reconciling the world to himself in Christ, not counting people's sins against them. And he has committed to us the message of reconciliation. We are therefore Christ's ambassadors, as though God were making his appeal through us. We implore you on Christ's behalf: Be reconciled to God. God made him who had no sin to be sin for us, so that in him we might become the righteousness of God.* (2 Cor. 5 NIV)

Because of this act of "Atonement," God's image-bearers can shine once again. The old has been swept away by the ministry of reconciliation. The truest destiny is that we are to become God's ambassadors to this world and examples of his righteousness. This is the life we are being called into. This is the truest story ever told. The ancient mythmakers always dreamed of a Father who would show his children how to transcend life and glimpse the all-encompassing power of the universe. They were looking for the perfect fatherly initiator. Jesus enters the scene and says that the Father is not a symbol of empty longing. He is the living God of the Universe. We are now reconciled, and when we pray to him, we can call him Father, or "Abba."

Difficult Advice

While Jesus offers the path to Atonement, he doesn't intend for us to watch and worship from afar. He gives some challenging instructions about how we are to approach the Supreme Ordeals in our own stories: "Whoever wants to be my disciple must deny themselves and take up their cross and follow me. For whoever wants to save their life will lose it, but whoever loses their life for me will find it." (Matt. 16:24-25 NIV)

This is the most difficult part of the journey to understand because Jesus's instructions to deny ourselves and lose our life run against all instincts of self-preservation. It may sound good when Jesus says it, but in application it's counterintuitive to everything we have learned and seen about how to survive in this world. Taking up the Cross and dying to ourselves is more than making sacrifices like volunteering, donating or giving up eating a certain food during Lent. At this point in the journey, we are traversing the deep emotional and spiritual territories that hold us back from living life wholeheartedly, and secure in the Father's love.

In the instructions from Jesus quoted above, the word translated as "life" (as in lose your life to find it) is translated from the Greek word *psychen* from which we derive English words such as *psychological* and *psyche*.[1] It has a connotation that means one's identity, personality or unique selfhood. Alternatively, we might also interpret Jesus's instructions as "if you want to find out who you really are, then you have to sacrifice who you think you are."

To understand this perplexing problem of identity or self-conception, we have to go back to the beginning, back to the story of the "Fall." Let us consider Adam and Eve as archetypes of humanity, the pattern from which we are all stamped. If we want to understand our story, we can simply look at what happens in this story—perhaps the most profound and simple explanation of human psychology ever written. Like any great myth, its eternal truth points beyond history. It explains the setting of our ordinary world and the starting point of our Hero's Journey.

The story of the Fall begins by telling us that "Adam and Eve were both naked, and they felt no shame." (Gen 2:25 NIV) The serpent comes and tempts them into eating from the forbidden tree. And the first thing they do after partaking of the forbidden fruit is go and hide their nakedness with fig leaves. That they were naked before the Fall and not naked after should be highlighted. When God comes looking for them, he calls on Adam. Here is how Adam responds:

"I heard you in the garden, and I was afraid because I was naked; so I hid." (Gen 3:10 NIV)

What happened at the Fall is that fear entered the world and along with it, shame (we will talk about sin in the next chapter). Notice Adam doesn't say he is afraid of God, the serpent or Eve. He says he is afraid of being naked. This is an unexpected and significant twist. Nakedness is the physical reality of what would best be described as a condition of vulnerability. Adam's fear centers on his vulnerability. He feels ashamed. He discovers that he is exposed, and he hides. This is where our story starts, in a condition of fear. Adam and Eve's response is our response, too. Our shame forces us to hide the areas of our life and personality that make us feel vulnerable.

Notable relationship researcher and author, Brené Brown, defines shame as the "intensely painful feeling or experience of believing that we are flawed and therefore unworthy of love and belonging—something we've experienced, done or failed to do makes us unworthy of connection."[2] The point of AT-ONE-MENT is to restore connection with the Father in order to believe, despite all that has happened in our life, we are worthy of love and belonging. The AT-ONE-MENT with the Father frees us to bear our vulnerability to others as well, and with that we may truly live. Our lives and relationships flourish the way they were intended before shame derailed us.

Our Crosses are the things in our lives that separate us from connection with the Father. It's rooted in our shame. Therefore, taking up our Cross requires us to abandon those false pretenses that protect us from feeling vulnerable. These are the things that are the limiting powers in our life, and we can't write our true story and complete our Hero's Journey without confronting them. We have to die to the ways in which we have protected ourselves from the fear of shame. They are undermining our marriages, friendships, parenting and relationship with God. We think the identity we are projecting to the outside world is helping us and keeping us safe, when in truth it's holding us captive.

Over the course of our life, we have all developed belief systems about how we can stand out and find significance. Traits like our insightfulness, humor, independence or many other such characteristics become the scaffolding from which we hang our identity. Our vulnerability without the assurance of the Father's love leads to one of three driving fears in our life: that we are alone, that we are exposed or that we are insignificant. So we respond by creating identities that attempt to stymie the fear and pain brought up by our vulnerability.

Somewhere deep down in our subconscious we think if we make more acquaintances and spend countless hours interacting on social media, we won't feel so alone. Or we think if we keep to ourselves and shut down as many emotions as possible, we won't feel exposed. We can lock our heart away and never get hurt. Or we think if we become a prominent business person and make a lot of money, we won't feel insignificant.

The traits and characteristics we have most identified with often have their source in the defining emotional traumas we have experienced during our life. The ones from early on, before we have an adult perspective to interpret things accurately, hold particular weight. Maturing as a Hero requires growing up in the areas that we have shut down because of the pain we experienced without a mature filter to understand it.

Our foundational belief system becomes corrupted by seeking our identity outside the Father's love. Instead of pursuing a life of significance, we focus on building a life to protect an identity we aren't convinced is real. Then we wonder why we feel like we are frauds or live in constant fear we will be discovered and the truth that we are stupid, weak, unlovable, alone or whatever other lie we are telling ourselves will be revealed.

Instead of living out of deep desire, we try to follow the script we think everyone else is expecting from us and then wonder why we feel so halfhearted about the things we do every day, always wondering why we can't find our true calling or why no amount of success fills the void. Instead of loving without reservation, we love with a host of protective barriers and caveats. We haven't accepted who we are because we don't know if we can trust the Father's love, so we can't fully open ourselves to others.

Blaise Pascal summed this up well, "We do not content ourselves with the life we have in ourselves and in our own being; we desire to live an imaginary life in the mind of others, and for this purpose we endeavor to shine. We labor unceasingly to adorn and preserve this imaginary existence, and neglect the real."[3] All of this need for projecting a false image of ourselves happens mostly below the surface of our awareness. It comes from the lies we believe about ourselves that are so deeply ingrained, we aren't even aware of their power over us.

How do we respond to this fear of being alone, insignificant or exposed? We adopt any number of false personas. We adopt character traits we believe will help keep us safe or make us feel important and respected. We turn to sports or hobbies for our purpose. We wrap our identities around our family, our church or ministry, our children and their performance. We seek identity in what we own or where we work.

The challenging part about identity is that the things we turn to can be positive or noble pursuits on the surface. They are the things about us that have gotten the most positive attention from others or make us feel most secure. The problem is that when we pursue anything in order to project a persona that we have created to fill a void, we are asking too much of the persona. We think it will bring us joy, fulfillment and life, but it lets us down every time.

A proper Hero's Journey will require us to confront our fears of vulnerability and will bring us face to face with the ingrained ways of relating to the world and the deep psychological limits placed on us by the way we have tried to protect ourselves from feeling alone, exposed or insignificant. Even though death in this phase may be is metaphorical, it's still painful. "There is no coming to consciousness without pain. People will do anything, no matter how absurd, in order to avoid facing their own soul," writes Carl Jung.[4]

There is a story C. S. Lewis tells in his book, *The Voyage of the Dawn Treader*, which effectively dramatizes this process of losing one's life to find it. The story is about a boy named Eustace who comes into possession of a large fortune. Sitting amongst his trove of treasure, Eustace puts a large gold bracelet around his arm and imagines the life and comforts he is going to enjoy. He falls asleep, dreaming about his newfound riches, but when he awakes he has turned into a dragon, an outward manifestation of his greed and selfishness. The bracelet he had put on is constricting his large, scaly, dragon leg, creating a piercing pain. Even worse, Eustace realizes that as a dragon he is isolated and alone.

As he begins to weep, Aslan, the Lion and Father-God figure of the story, shows up and leads Eustace to a well on top of a mountain. Eustace thinks if he can get himself into the well, the cool water will sooth the pain in his leg. But Aslan tells Eustace that he must undress first. After a moment of confusion, Eustace realizes Aslan means he must shed his scaly skin the way a snake does. Baring his dragon claws, he tears at the skin but discovers there is another layer of skin below the first one. He tears at the next layer, only to discover another layer below that. He realizes his efforts to remove the skin and find the relief he seeks is pointless. Eustace describes what happens next as Aslan comes closer:

> Then the lion said, "You will have to let me undress you." I was afraid of his claws, I can tell you, but I was pretty nearly desperate now. So I just lay flat down on my back to let him do it.
>
> The very first tear he made was so deep that I thought it had gone right into my heart. And when he began pulling the skin off, it hurt worse than anything I've ever felt. The only thing that made me able to bear it was just the pleasure of feeling the stuff peel off. You know — if you've ever picked the scab of a sore place. It hurts like billy-oh but it is such fun to see it coming away."
>
> Well, he peeled the beastly stuff right off —just as I thought I'd done it myself the other three times, only they hadn't hurt— and there it was lying on the grass, only ever so much thicker, and darker, and more knobbly-looking than the others had been. And there was I smooth and soft as a peeled switch and smaller than I had been. Then he caught hold of me—I didn't like that much for I was very tender underneath now that I'd no skin on—and threw me into the water. It smarted like anything but only for a moment. After that it became perfectly delicious and as soon as I started swimming and splashing I found that all the

pain had gone from my arm. And then I saw why. I'd turned into a boy again.... [5]

Our self-constructed identities are like Eustace's scales. We think they are protecting us, but they are really just projections of deeper issues, cutting us off from connection with others. The path to freedom is submission to the Father; we must lay down our life and let the Father redefine us through his love. What we sacrifice, our self-protected skin, feels like part of us and so it may not be pleasant—"it might smart like anything but only for a moment," but the reward will be freedom, wholeness and authentic connections to others. We might think of ourselves as a beautiful creature, but we are a dragon compared to the way we could be if we trusted the Father's love enough to lie down in front of him and let him undress the hideous skin, the false personas, we thought were protecting us.

Identifying the Ordeals in Our Journey

The presence of fear is probably the best clue that we might be approaching the Supreme Ordeal of the Hero's Journey, especially if the level of fear seems to be an overreaction to the potential risk involved. We might say to ourselves, "I shouldn't fear this as much as I do." We can rationalize why a particular risk shouldn't seem so frightening, but what we convince our head to believe doesn't seem to help the emotional response we are feeling. This is the point in the journey where our courage will be tested the most. We come to a decision to push through and respond to the Supreme Ordeal the way we always have, out of a false persona, or we can take a risk and try a new approach.

Let's say the Call to Adventure right now is that we work on our marriage, and let's say our spouse tells us that he or she believes we have prioritized a hobby or a career over our family. We disagree at first, and that isn't our intent. However, when we look at the actions of our life, we realize that our spouse has a point. The Supreme Ordeal could be giving up the hobby or career path for a season, or longer. If our identity is wrapped around hobbies or career, giving them up or lessening their importance will feel like losing a part of ourselves.

It won't feel safe and will make us feel vulnerable (to being alone, exposed or insignificant). We will be tempted to make up all kinds of rationalizations for why this isn't a good idea or why our spouse is wrong. But deep down, if we are honest, we find that our rationalizations are all driven to help us avoid facing the fear wrought by the suggestion.

Sharing a part of our story that we have never shared before might be the Supreme Ordeal confronting us. We might have a dark secret from the past. Maybe it's something we did. Maybe it's something that was done to us. Maybe it's something that we are still doing. Nevertheless, it holds a tremendous amount of weight in our life. We don't readily admit that because we have put great effort into covering the hole that this part of our story has left in our heart. We have worked hard to shut that part of our heart down. But as long as this secret stays in the dark, it retains its power. Only by bringing it into the light will we be able to finally address this part of our story that has never been fully addressed. If you, the reader, have a secret that you have never confronted in your life, your heart is probably racing as you read this. You may be tempted to put the book down right now. It's terrifying stuff.

I believe that, for me, writing this book is a type of Hero's Journey. It's not the first or most significant one, but I can already see how it has brought about new perspective and insights. I wish I could see clearly what lies ahead, but that's difficult in the midst of the trials. I can only guess what the Atonement might entail for me. Perhaps it will be the day I publish this book and share with the world what I have written. Writing a book has its own challenges, but sending it out for public consumption may be the most difficult step psychologically. As I write this, I am still free from the judgment and criticism of others. That will change when I share it. That's when I will really be exposed. I could be wrong; maybe publishing is just another step in the Road of Trials and something more challenging than publishing is actually what lies ahead. I'll just have to wait and see what happens.

Freed by Love

Joseph Campbell said the ultimate symbol of life was Jesus's crucifixion, and Campbell wasn't a Christian. The crucifixion is the symbol of the ultimate sacrifice, which is another way of saying it's the ultimate symbol of love. The crucifixion (or Atonement) communicates that love has conquered death, and since the fear of death is the greatest fear, the crucifixion means that love has conquered fear as well. It's only when we have freedom from the fear of death, both real and metaphorical, that we are truly free to live. If we want to understand the truth about the Father's love, the crucifixion offers the evidence. If we want to conquer the things that have held ultimate power over us, the crucifixion offers the prescription. Atonement, or At-One-Ment, goes beyond just becoming more like the Father; it also means At-One-Ment with our authentic identities.

Real life, as opposed to fictional stories, requires us to continually take different Hero's Journeys. Not all of them reach a point that can be labeled a life-and-death struggle. Some atoning acts require small sacrifices, whereas others bring about an existential crisis. What matters is that each successful journey reveals a little more of our true character and personality to the world. Another helpful metaphor is something Michelangelo said about carving his famous statue of David. When asked about his creative process, Michelangelo said, "I saw the angel in the marble and carved until I set him free." Michelangelo started with a twenty-foot slab of Carrara marble and chipped away to reveal one of the most magnificent works of art in the history of the world. I think this quote also relates to the potential in each of us. We are locked away inside an unformed block of marble, and every time we take the Hero's Journey, a piece of marble gets carved away, revealing a little bit of the masterpiece inside. Some journeys may only take a nick out of the marble. Other journeys lop off large sections, revealing entire features of our unique identities.

When we hear Jesus's instruction that we must lose our life to find it, we may be tempted to think of this in terms of losing our distinctness, calling for some undifferentiated and unremarkable state of existence. But the reincarnation suggests that we are far more than we think we are. Joseph Campbell discussed how limited the self-conception of the uninitiated individual is: "There are dimensions of your being and a potential for realization and consciousness that are not included in your concept of yourself. Your life is much deeper and broader than you conceive it to be here. What you are living is but a fractional inkling of what is really within you, what gives you life, breadth."[6] We are all David locked in the marble. What we will look like when we emerge is what we will explore in the following chapters as we turn to the outcome of the Atonement with the Father and the completion of our initiation as Heroes.

CHAPTER XI

REWARDS

IN JOSEPH CAMPBELL'S BOOK, *Hero with a Thousand Faces*, he identified two phases that occur as the result of the Atonement. First, the Hero experiences a transition to a higher self—what Campbell labeled "Apotheosis." In mythology apotheosis is the idea of raising an individual to a godlike nature. In addition to this metamorphosis from one nature to the another, the Hero gets his reward, the Ultimate Boon. Because these two resulting phases of the Atonement are so closely related, I will cover them together in this chapter.

Apotheosis

In this phase the Hero attains a divine state as he comes to understand that the Everlasting lives within him. The ego is finally set aside as the desires of his previously uninitiated state are left behind. He is free to enjoy the bounty of living in communion with the Father and as part of the Father. Peace is achieved because the Hero is now in a place to receive the spiritual blessings of one who has faced the ordeals of setting his selfish desires and ambitions aside. Time and eternity are no longer disparate experiences; they are connected. Death is not the end of life; it's the beginning of life's renewal.

Ultimate Boon

All of the previous steps have prepared the Hero for this final step before beginning his return. Here the Hero finally achieves the goal of his quest and gets his reward. He finds the magic elixir he has been seeking—the image of indestructibility is finally realized. In some cases, if the Hero is ready, the boon allows the Hero to transcend the limits of his own understanding and personality. He gains perfect illumination. He is at one with the heavens, and he convenes with a light and vision that goes well beyond the limits of what we could describe or portray with human words or pictures. He has penetrated to the source of life itself and has received a gift that makes all of the trials faced on his journey worthwhile.

WE HAVE REACHED THE POINT in the journey where the hero experiences the reward of the quest. He has cheated death and seized the sword. In storytelling the prize may take various forms. It might come as an epiphany, in which the Hero sees the truth behind a deception and experiences a moment of divine recognition. The Hero might gain special powers of insight, intuition or self-actualization. The Hero might be crowned, knighted or find the Holy Grail. Sometimes the reward is love itself.

Dorothy gets her reward in *The Wizard of Oz* when she wins the broomstick she has been challenged to steal. In *The Lord of the Rings*, Frodo reaches Mount Doom and destroys the ring, thereby defeating the evil spirit of Sauron and rescuing Middle-earth. In the *Matrix* Neo confronts the agents, an encounter that no one else has ever survived. Neo believes he will have to sacrifice his life to save his mentor Morpheus's life. In the process of facing death, Neo discovers he is the chosen one, and he is able to transcend the limitations of his previous self-conception.

Jesus Achieves His Mission

One of the first stops Jesus makes after returning from his trials in the wilderness and launching his public ministry is his hometown of Nazareth. He goes into the synagogue on the Sabbath. The entire town is there. Jesus walks to the front of the crowd, unrolls a scroll and reads a passage from the prophet Isaiah written many generations earlier:

> *The Spirit of the Sovereign Lord is on me,*
> *because the Lord has anointed me*
> *to proclaim good news to the poor.*
> *He has sent me to bind up the brokenhearted,*

to proclaim freedom for the captives
and release from darkness for the prisoners. (Is. 61:1 NIV)

Everyone listening in the synagogue would have been familiar with this passage of scripture. They had been reading it with hope for centuries, waiting expectantly for the Messiah to arrive. When Jesus finishes reading, he rolls the scroll back up. Slowly and deliberately he surveys the room. He pauses and hands the scroll back to the attendant. Every eye in the synagogue is on him. He sits down and still everyone is waiting for him. Then he says what to their ears must have seemed outrageous: "Today this scripture is fulfilled in your hearing." This man whom the people of Nazareth have known since he was a child and watched grow up is claiming to be the fulfillment of their greatest hope.

Why does Jesus choose to read from the prophet Isaiah? Because he is framing his mission: to give good news to the poor, freedom to the prisoners and sight to the blind. He means this literally. His next four years of ministry will be marked by miracles of the blind seeing and the poor being uplifted by his message. But the words he quotes are also figurative, describing the human condition before the completion of Jesus's mission. When he says he is here for the poor, blind, brokenhearted prisoners, he is talking about all of us. This is what he accomplishes, on behalf of those listening in that Nazarene synagogue 2,000 years ago and the rest of the world.

Fast forward a few years from this proclamation. Jesus is on the Cross. It's three in the afternoon, and darkness has come over the entire land. The curtain of the temple is torn in two. Bloody, exhausted and slowly dying, Jesus is praying. Finally, he gasps and calls out, "Father, into your hands I commit my spirit." (Luke 23:46 NIV) And having said that he breathed his last. He will return three days later in a resurrected body, but he has accomplished his mission. By sacrificing himself on the Cross, he has paved the way for the Atonement of all heroes. He didn't just "save us from our sins." He did far more. He sets us free from the bondage of living out of fear and shame. He heals our brokenness and gives us sight to see our own lives and God's eternal story clearly. He replaces oppression with love.

Everything changes when he breathes his last breath. His reward is our freedom. He has lowered himself down as a man and has taken on the limits of human nature. Through his sacrifice on the Cross he has overcome that nature—not just for himself but for everyone.

The Fruit of the Journey

The reward for surviving the Supreme Ordeal in our own real-life Hero's Journey might come in the form of tangible accomplishments or experiences we set out to achieve. We might start a new business, survive the trials of the first year and finally make our first monthly profit, raise money or ship our first product. We might dedicate a year to writing a book, spend months getting rejected by potential publishers and find the hidden treasure when a publisher agrees to publish our work. We might decide to pursue formal education in a new field and receive our crown in the form of a graduation cap. We might begin a new romantic relationship and for the first time set aside all of the self-protecting mechanisms that have led to our ultimate isolation in the past. The relationship doesn't end this time. A ring on the finger symbolizes it's just beginning.

These tangible rewards reflect a more important transformation that has taken place internally. More often than not, the reward is something that isn't immediately obvious to the outside world. The most important outcome of the quest is how our belief systems change. We come to a better understanding of who we are and our unique purpose on this planet. We don't rush around trying to impress others because we now feel secure in the love of a heavenly Father. We aren't confused by the chaos of life. Instead, we're settled and rooted. We walk freely and lightly in the same situations that threaten to crush the uninitiated with their burden. We have experienced truth that has allowed us to transcend our previously limited views of life.

When we have faced the fear of our vulnerability and have replaced it with the perfecting love of God, the Father, amazing things happen: Situations change, relationships improve and dreams are realized. With each successful Supreme Ordeal, we find that the winds of destiny begin to work on our side. And what is destiny? It's what happens when "God-given desires, mixed with a person's particular gifting are healed, matured and released so that they can be freely given away." [1]

For the duration of this chapter, we will turn our attention to three areas of inner-life transformation that occur as a result of a successful Hero's Journey. A Hero who has endured will find his life will become characterized by greater fulfillment, wholeness and rest.

Fulfillment

Erik Liddell was a Scottish born Olympic runner immortalized in the classic movie, *Chariots of Fire*. The movie follows Liddell and his English rival, Harold Abrahams, as they both train to qualify for the 1924 Olympics. The story reveals that while each man might appear to be chasing the same goal (Olympic Gold medal), their motives for running are entirely different. Abrahams runs to feed his own ego and is tormented by his compulsion to win. Liddell runs because he loves to run.

During the movie Liddell's sister, who is deeply religious, tells him it's time he think about bringing his running career to a close. She believes her brother should join her as a missionary in China. Liddell is not convinced, and he responds to his sister's prodding, "I believe God made me for a purpose. But he also made me fast. And when I run I feel his pleasure." Liddell reorients what most religious people think of as pleasing God. Instead, he is doing what he was born to do, enjoying his unique gift and worshiping God by simply running.

Both Liddell and Abrahams go on to win Olympic Gold medals. In fact, in the face of tremendous pressure to discount his beliefs, Liddell withdraws from his best event (the 100-meter race) because it is scheduled for Sunday (the Sabbath), a day he has reserved for worshiping God. He wins the 400-meter race instead. Abrahams is let down at the end of the movie when he wins his Olympic Gold medal. All of those years chasing the Gold medal to satisfy his own ego have made the victory hollow, echoing his thought from earlier in the movie when he says, "I'm forever in pursuit and I don't even know what I am chasing."

Abrahams has succumbed to the great fallacy of our modern culture that the achievements born out of a desire to prove our own significance and value will satisfy us. But they never do. They keep us forever in pursuit, always leaping out ahead of us so that as soon as we scale one mountain, we discover there is yet still another, greater mountain to scale.

Like Abrahams, we don't even know what we are chasing, so we follow the culture. We do what everyone else does yet expect different results. Maybe we can relate to what author Ellen Goodman describes as the ordinary world for most people today: "Normal is getting dressed in clothes that you buy for work and driving through traffic in a car that you are still paying for ... in order to get to the job that you need to pay for the clothes and the car and the house you leave vacant all day so you can afford to live in it." Thoreau put it this way: "The mass of men lead lives of quiet desperation, and go to the grave with the song still in them."

The Atonement, the dying of our old identity, frees us to experience a more fulfilled existence. When we don't live to prove our worth to others, or to God, because that doubt is no longer in question, then our calling becomes clear and so do our desires. We can run like Erik Liddell, or we can pursue our career, marriage, hobbies or friendships with the same passionate freedom as Erik Liddell. God made us for a purpose, too. We may not be as fast as Erik Liddell, but we are something. And when we find what that something is and use our God-given desires without reservation about how others will perceive them, the reward is fulfillment.

There is often an unspoken pressure in church culture to make the purpose of life about duty and behavior. Things get measured by their perceived ministerial value. Liddell's sister wants him to give up running so that he can move his life to more spiritually important matters. But she has missed the point. Jesus said, "Behold the Kingdom of God is within you." Worship is a state of the heart, and nothing makes the heart dance and sing like the liberation of our desires as they meet our unique gifts. When our heart exists in this state of freedom, then everything, even running, can take on a form of worship and fulfillment.

Perhaps we might move to China and become a missionary as Liddell eventually did after the 1924 Olympics, but that is not the point. I think the idea of having to give up everything for some ministry activity scares a lot of would-be Heroes from surrendering to the Call to Adventure that the Father is inviting them to accept. They're afraid if they do, God will make them sell everything they own, homeschool their children and move to a remote village in Papua New Guinea. But what we learn through the Hero's Journey is that the Father isn't trying to get us to live a life we don't want to live. He's trying to help us find the life we always wanted but has eluded us because we have never faced the fears and gone through the process of restoration that we discussed in the previous chapter. There is a chasm between who we are and who we want to be. Closing that gap doesn't happen by substituting striving in one area of our life with striving in another area of our life, even if that other area is deemed "spiritual" or gets the approval of the church culture. The emptiness doesn't go away, and we actually don't become more spiritual. We just become more religious and there is a big difference between those two things.

In his book, Man's Search for Meaning, psychologist and holocaust survivor Viktor Frankl said that modern man lives in an "existential vacuum," vacillating between two extremes: distress and boredom. He writes, "Boredom is now causing, and certainly bringing to psychiatrists, more problems to solve than distress.... Let us consider, for instance, "Sunday neurosis," that kind of depression which afflicts people who become aware of the lack of content in their lives when the rush of the busy week is over and the void within themselves becomes manifest. Not a few cases of suicide can be traced back to this existential vacuum. Such widespread phenomena as depression, aggression and addiction are not understandable unless we recognize the existential vacuum underlying them."[2]

If we don't have a crisis occupying our attention, we have a tendency toward boredom, and Monday might become a daunting and depressing prospect. I know more than a few people who seem to find comfort in creating chaos in their lives. You probably know people like this, too. They overcommit, have no time, make hasty decisions and are always complaining (or bragging) about how busy and hectic life is.

They stay in this cycle for years and you wonder, "Why do they always do this to themselves?" Maybe you wonder why you do this to yourself. The answer is that they prefer to remain in distress than to slow down long enough to sense the existential vacuum that creates the conditions for Sunday neurosis and other ailments.

The other option is to relieve the boredom with any variety of small idols and little pleasures, which tend to grow into bigger idols and pleasures. One more glass of wine becomes one more bottle. Watching one television episode turns into a three-day binge. A short time spent on social media ends when we reach the bottom of the Internet. We fill the margins of life before we have to think too hard about why we are here on this earth to begin with.

Not to diminish a good glass of wine, but we are tempted to settle for far too little. "It would seem that our Lord finds our desires not too strong, but too weak," writes C. S. Lewis. "We are half-hearted creatures, fooling about with drink and sex and ambition when infinite joy is offered us, like an ignorant child who wants to go on making mud pies in a slum because he cannot imagine what is meant by the offer of a holiday at the sea. We are far too easily pleased."[3]

Small pleasures don't satisfy the Hero. He doesn't live in an endless cycle between distress and boredom. This is his reward for answering the Call to Adventure, seeking his SuperNatural aid and traversing the trials and ordeals in his path. The Hero closes the chasm between the life he desires and the life he is living. He discovers his real identity and lets others see his vulnerability. He writes his story with a sense of fulfillment.

Wholeness

No one skates through life without getting hurt. The Hero hasn't avoided suffering either; he has taken his lumps, too. Our false personas exist to cover up a fragmented heart and protect it from further damage. Living in Atonement, under the Father's love, also offers the Hero wholeness. By confronting those great fears surrounding his identity, the Hero allows his wounds to be healed, and his heart is put back together. Jesus promised when he announced his mission,

"I have come to bind up the brokenhearted." (Is 61:1 NIV) In all of those hurt and scared places the Hero is being healed by the perfecting love of the Father. He has set aside his self-protective defenses and has surrendered to a greater identity and truer story. He is becoming whole.

We all need healing from emotional and spiritual traumas. Mankind was created in the image of God, but for a variety of reasons, that reflection has been warped. We were cut off from the relationship required to experience the Father's love. Jesus's Atonement paves the way for the restoration of the connection, and as a result the various shards of our heart that split off during the course of life may be healed and reintegrated. In the process, the quality of our life begins to reflect that of Jesus's.

When I mentioned the Fall in the previous chapter, I pointed out that fear and shame entered the picture during that time. But I didn't mention sin, which is what usually gets discussed in the retelling of the Adam and Eve's story. I didn't cover it then because I don't think sin is the Supreme Ordeal or Atonement of our Journey (at least in the way most people think of sin). Less sin (or said in the positive, more holiness), is the reward of the Atonement—not a requirement for it.

The original sin of Adam and Eve was this: they doubted the Father's love. They thought maybe he was holding out on them, so they fell to the temptation of eating from the forbidden tree. They thought maybe they would be better off doing things their way, and that created the conditions for all the other things we might label sin. This is the battle we fight, too. We doubt the provisions of the Father's love. We wonder if God even exists. If he exists, does he care? If he cares, could he possibly be pleased with who we are? Or is he just a malevolent force? We struggle with living in AT-ONE-MENT with the Father, so we live as Adam and Eve did, taking things into our own hands just in case. Which means we try to manage through life with the haunting fear we are alone, exposed or insignificant. And these fears are the root of sin in our lives.

As an example, let's take a rampant problem in our society such as sex addiction and pornography. What is the cause? I know more than a few guys who have struggled earnestly with the addiction to pornography in their lives. They hate it, and their inability to resist it isn't from a lack of effort or desire to be free. Trying harder, accountability programs and guilt have not worked. I think one reason so many men have difficulty resisting pornography is because it makes them feel like a man without requiring them to act like one. Pornography is a short-term fix to the fear that most men have about their identity and the gnawing question of "whether they have what it takes."[4]

Pornography is a goddess a man will bow to and worship in order to feel validated and loved. The goddess stands in for a minute and delivers temporarily. But the ultimate effect is that the man ends up feeling even less like a man and even more alone and exposed. In pornography long-term wholeness is traded for short-term relief. Indulging only serves to reinforce the underlying motive for indulging (not feeling worthy of love), which makes the sin even harder to resist the next time temptation presents itself creating a cycle that feeds itself.

Let's take a less noticeable sin such as judgment, something we may fall into without even realizing it. Where does a judgmental spirit come from? We may be scrolling our social media accounts before bed, and before long we're feeling inferior and left out. We wonder why everyone else lives more interesting lives than we do. As we continue to compare ourselves with others, we begin to wish we could take more exotic vacations, have more friends or wear trendier clothes. Old wounds are activated by the same messages we have been hearing our entire life: we're alone, insignificant and exposed. Then the subconscious kicks in to protect us. Judgment is our weapon of choice to confront the situation. We scroll through our favorite social media account and pick out our first target for ridicule. If we can diminish this person enough in our mind, then it will give us some relief from how we are feeling about ourselves. We begin to judge and criticize in our mind. But just as with porn or any other sin, the result is only temporary relief. In the long run, the judgment doesn't make us feel any better about ourselves. It does nothing to address the core fear. Also, it makes us less accepting of others, perpetuating and reinforcing one of the very things that we feared to begin with: we are alone.

Ultimately, sin is a response to fear. I believe original sin might also be labeled "original fear." The fear we feel from being outside the protection of an all-powerful love is the oxygen that sin needs to inflame our lives, which means that, if we want to defeat sin, then we have to somehow confront the central fear that draws us toward pornography, the protective walls of judgment or any other sin. The Gospel writer, John, offers the ultimate solution: "There is no fear in love." Instead, he writes, "Perfect love drives out fear. The one who fears is not made perfect in love." (1 John 4:18) This is the antidote to fear—coming under the perfecting power of the Father's love. Fear and love cannot coexist.

How do we come into this perfect power of love? We surrender our identities that have protected us. We bear our Cross as Jesus did and endure the necessary ordeals. As we do this, fear loses its authority in our lives, and because of that, so does sin. The Hero becomes whole, not in order to please the Father, but because he discovers he already does. A Hero's Journey that takes the defeat of sin as its core mission has missed the point. Jesus's Atonement dealt with our sin for us. God has not only forgiven our sins but also has already forgotten them (Heb. 8:12). That we are as pure as Jesus is already the way the Father sees us. Any attempt to earn love through our behavior is a denial of Jesus's atoning work and a twisted form of pride.

Of course, Jesus's work doesn't excuse us to go on sinning unrepentantly. That perspective misses the point even more. The objective is not to clean up the behavior, but to become the type of person who is less and less a slave to sin. That is what the Hero's Journey is about and what the Atonement phase raises in particular. To enter the promise of becoming a new creation and by learning to come under the Father's grace, we find it is true what Paul wrote: we are no longer a slave to sin but a slave to righteousness. The Hero is whole, and because of that he is far better equipped to deal with the sin of the world. He doesn't operate out of guilt and obligations as much as he operates out of inspiration. He knows who he is and who he wants to become, and, as a result, he finds old sins less and less appealing.

Rest

The modern world can be an exhausting place to live in. We're connected to every instance of breaking news from every corner of the earth by means of a device that resides in our pockets and sits on a table next to our beds. E-mails, texts, instant messages and tweets bombard us at all hours. It seems like everyone is trying to outdo the next person—trying to get ahead in our careers, never missing a social event, planning our children's college admission application before they are out of the womb. The culture tells us, when in doubt, go bigger, newer and shinier. Strive... Strive ... Strive!

Heaven forbid we hit a speed bump at the blinding pace demanded of us today. Most of us are already weary enough. What do we do when we add to the mix an ailing and aging parent who needs care, a recession in our industry, a child who is getting bullied, a health problem, a marriage problem, a drinking problem and so on? A rapid pace and a heavy burden is the rule, not the exception for modern life.

The Hero's Journey is arduous, but the Hero also learns how to rest along the way. He doesn't have to strive because he is no longer a slave to the opinion of others. He is comfortable with himself. He doesn't have to deal with the exhaustion of pretending he is someone he is not. He no longer subjects himself to halfhearted pursuits in an effort to please others. What this means in practical terms is that the Hero spends more time on things that bring him life and energize his spirit and less time on the activities and concerns that drain and wear him down.

Most of us over-commit because we can't say no. And we can't say no because we don't know what our purpose is. Nor are we clear about our true desires. Clarity of purpose brings conviction about how we should focus our time and energy. As a result, we say no to the things that distract us from our purpose. If we don't know what we want, we don't know when to say no. Instead, we keep saying yes because we fear missing out or don't want to disappoint others. We say yes too many times. We overcommit, and it's exhausting.

The Hero can also rest because he has a place for the burdens that come as part of life. He knows he doesn't have to carry them alone.

The journey has taught him how to navigate the trials and ordeals that are a part of all great stories. The Hero has learned to call on his SuperNatural aid, the Holy Spirit, to help him. He has experienced the reality of this force in his life and knows he can count on it when times become difficult. The Hero has also discovered the grace that comes from the Father's love. He has experienced the transforming power of that love to bring redemption from even the most painful wounds and trying circumstances. He can rest that "God works everything out for those who love him." (Rom 8:28 NIV) He knows this isn't an empty promise because he has already experienced it firsthand.

The Hero knows rest is essential. Even God rested. The Hero is determined that he will not allow the world's incessant demands to dictate the pace of his life. He can carry a great burden without it crushing him because he has learned he doesn't have to carry it alone.

The Gift of the Journey

In his best-selling novel, *The Alchemist*, Paulo Coelho chronicles the quest of an Andalusian shepherd boy named Santiago. One night while camping with his sheep in an old abandoned church, Santiago has a recurring dream he believes to be prophetic. The dream leads Santiago on an adventure from the old church in Spain to the pyramids of Egypt in search of a treasure he is sure his dream is leading him to find. The journey is full of trials, mentors and temptations—a classic Hero's Journey. But Santiago's quest ends with an ironic twist. He discovers that the treasure he has been seeking is not out in the desert of Egypt. It's buried under the old church where he first had the dream that called him to the adventure. He asks, "Why should I travel for so long just to find what is near?" He gets his answer from the wind: "If I had told you, you wouldn't have seen the pyramids. They're beautiful, aren't they?"

The real treasure of the journey is not what is buried at the church. It wasn't an accomplishment or the attainment of some possession. The treasure is the experience of following his dreams, and in doing so, he has experienced beauty, love and adventure—things he would never have discovered had he simply woken up from his dream and dug up the treasure under where he had slept. Santiago's reward is not gold; it's what he has learned about himself and the transformative effect of pursuing his dreams despite the risks and setbacks experienced along the way. *The Wizard of Oz* ends with a similar twist. Dorothy discovers that to get home, all she has to do is click the heels together of her ruby slippers. She had the means of getting home with her all along, but she couldn't see the truth until she had lived through the adventure. If she had discovered this at the beginning, she would have been cheated out of her story and so would we.

I think these lessons are no less true for us. It's easy to fixate on the destination and forget that life is happening now and that it's often the simplest things that are the most extraordinary. We think if we can just attain some goal, accomplish some difficult task, make a great sum of money, find the right partner, we will be able to finally stop and enjoy things. But we are disappointed when we get the treasure we sought only to find it doesn't offer the fulfillment and joy we thought it would. We move to the next thing we hope will fill the void, never stopping to consider why this cycle doesn't seem to be working. The ruby slippers have been on our feet all along. The treasure is right beneath where we sleep. It's inside our hearts—carefully and lovingly placed there by our Heavenly Father. We may come to him unashamed and open ourselves to experiences we may have not noticed otherwise. Life may take on a new quality, where our pursuits bring fulfillment and purpose, where a wholeness and holiness permeate our character and inner life, and we experience renewal instead of being worn down to the bone by the speed and burden of modern life.

CHAPTER XII

RETURN

Magic Flight

As the Hero attempts to return to his Ordinary World, he may encounter further resistance in his attempted departure. If the reward has been won against an opposition or a guardian of the Ultimate Boon, the Hero may find himself being pursued during his return. A chase of sorts may take place, and the Hero may have to utilize a variety of evasive techniques to escape those hoping to bar his return home.

THE HERO BEGAN THE JOURNEY in the Ordinary World, and now it's time to return, bringing the gifts he has gleaned during his travels to those characters he interacts with in daily life. But the journey back has its own trials, temptations and enemies. The resistance facing the Hero doesn't vanish because the Hero has experienced illumination and Atonement. The forces blocking the Hero's journey through the mystical world are desperate to prevent him from returning to inspire other would-be Heroes.

Joseph Campbell labeled this phase the "Magic Flight." The Hero must outwit and outrun his pursuers. In some cases an intervening force may need to rescue him. The Hero's SuperNatural aid may need to come to the rescue once again—a "Rescue from Without," in the parlance of the Hero's Journey. For example, after Frodo destroys the ring in the heart of Mount Doom, the mountain begins to crumble and spew volcanic lava. Frodo and his companion, Sam, run for their lives, dodging fiery debris and volcanic explosions. They don't get far before they find themselves stranded on an outcropping of rock in a sea of rising lava. Gandalf, Frodo's SuperNatural aid throughout the journey, brings a trio of eagles to rescue Frodo and Sam and bring them back to the Ordinary World.

The Hero may have to make additional sacrifices on the road back or may need to acknowledge once more that his old approaches and dependencies won't work. Dorothy gets her ticket home in the Wizard of Oz in the form of a hot air balloon ride with the Wizard of Oz. The people have gathered to see her off, but Dorothy's dog, Toto, sees a cat and chases it. Dorothy goes to retrieve Toto, and in the commotion the balloon that was to take her home becomes untethered and floats away. Dorothy is stuck again until the good witch Glinda shows up to point out that Dorothy has always had the capacity to get herself home. She doesn't need the Wizard and his tricks. In many movies the return is marked by a culminating chase scene as the Hero, with the help of a horse, car, spaceship or other mode of transportation, eludes the bad guys one last time.

In the biblical accounts of Jesus's journey, we have little information on what he did between his death on Good Friday and his return in a resurrected body three days later. There is one passage in a letter from Peter that offers a clue, suggesting that Jesus's return was also an adventure. Peter says Jesus was put to death in the body but made alive in the Spirit. "After being made alive, he went and made proclamation to the imprisoned spirits—to those who were disobedient long ago when God waited patiently in the days of Noah while the ark was being built." (1 Pet. 20 NIV) Evidently, between Jesus's Atonement and his resurrection, he had work to do. It included a stop to liberate those spirits who, from antiquity, had been held in prison. The Apostles' Creed says Jesus "descended into Hell" before returning. We won't venture into the debate about exactly what happened and whether the spirits Peter talks about were in Hell or somewhere else. I just want to point out that again Jesus is the quintessential Hero for us to emulate. On the Cross he says, "It is finished." (John 19:30 NIV) The Atonement had been won, but there remained a road back to the Ordinary World.

In our real world the old identities, habits, addictions and flaws won't relinquish their control of us easily. Despite our attempts to remove them, they may counterattack. We think we have passed them by to find they have only retreated temporarily. The Atonement has changed us, but the old flawed way of living can be deeply ingrained. We might slip back into an old well-worn identity. An addiction or habit we thought had been vanquished returns with a vengeance. We stumble into some new or old temptation. Our departing journey was difficult but the return journey may be difficult terrain as well. The real-world Hero's Journey is often messy and nonlinear. We might have to overcome the same obstacle multiple times. Even after the Atonement, we might experience periods of clairvoyance followed by moments of confusion. Darkness might descend in the wake of illumination.

The reality that the return may be marked by difficulty and times of failure doesn't invalidate the trip. It's easy to see why this can be discouraging. If we have battled our way through the Supreme Ordeal, experienced the transcendence of the Atonement and believe wholeheartedly that it has changed us permanently, a setback might come as quite a surprise. It might tempt us to conclude that our journey has not been authentic— it's just wishful thinking. If it's real, why do we continue to struggle with the same issues? We might feel like a hypocrite and open the door to the old fears of aloneness, insignificance and exposure, allowing them to exert their power over us once more.

As you return to the Ordinary World, take comfort that the Hero's Journey is not about becoming a finished product. We will never be a finished product on this earth. The Hero's Journey is a cycle, a continuous repetition of departure, initiation and return. Experiencing a return of challenges and struggles in areas from which we think we have gained freedom doesn't mean that we haven't done important work. It may just mean that we aren't complete yet. In some cases the fact that we face increased opposition after taking the sacrificial steps required to bring us to this point in the journey might be a sign of just how far we have come. It might reveal the threat for good that we pose if we are sustained in our Ordinary World with the rewards we have won. There is an enemy that wants nothing more than for us to fail, especially as we grow in authority by living authentically. What better way for an enemy to neutralize us as a threat than to convince us that we will never be free, that we are phonies and that the love of the Father is just wishful thinking. The struggle doesn't end because we have tasted freedom.

Crossing the Return Threshold

Ready to return from that other mystical place where the ego goes to die, the Hero faces one final ordeal. It is here that he is retested and fully cleansed so that he can be resurrected into ordinary life. As he crosses this final threshold, he must determine how to reintegrate himself into the world, which he may find bewildering at times. He must determine how to knit the two worlds of his experience—the temporal and eternal—together. He might find that his values have changed such that the distinctions that once seemed important have lost their appeal to him. He might find it difficult to relate to those who can only see the world of their senses and not what lies beyond, as the Hero has seen.

The Return Threshold can also be labeled the Resurrection. The Hero has died to a previous version of himself, and now he must be reborn into his Ordinary World. To be clear the journey might entail other moments of rebirth before the Resurrection back into the Ordinary World (or Crossing the Return Threshold). The Hero often experiences an initial transformation directly after departing the Ordinary World as he takes on the identity required to survive the Road of Trials that lies ahead. Campbell labeled the initial death-rebirth experience the "Belly of the Whale" phase. In Jesus's story the Belly of the Whale phase occurs at his baptism in the Jordan River. It's here the Holy Spirit descends on him like a dove and he crosses into the wilderness. Luke Skywalker has his Belly of the Whale experience when he, Hans Solo and Princess Leia have to escape the Stormtroopers and inadvertently find themselves stuck in the Death Star's trash compactor. The walls contract around them, and in the commotion a vile snake-like creature drags Luke beneath the watery waste. This is the first time Luke has faced the possibility of death and experiences a kind of baptism as he emerges from the liquid waste and frees himself from the creature. The first death-rebirth experience comes in recognition that the Hero has entered new territory (the field of adventure) and has been initiated into the mystical realm.

Crossing the Return Threshold marks the Hero's return from the field of adventure back into the Ordinary World. It's the final and culminating Resurrection of the Journey as the Hero brings the gifts of the adventure and newfound identity back to daily life. In *The Wizard of Oz*, Dorothy discovers she had the means to get home all along. Glinda instructs her to tap her heels together three times and repeat, "There is no place like home. There is no place like home."

She awakens in her room with her family and friends all around her. Was she asleep, unconscious or was the journey real? That's not the important point. What matters is that Dorothy has matured in her views of "home." Returning to consciousness back in Kansas signifies her rebirth. Acknowledging her new perspective on life she tells Glinda, "If I ever go looking for my heart's desire again, I won't go looking any farther than my own backyard."

After discovering he is the chosen one in the *Matrix*, Neo prevails in his encounter with one of the agents who hunt him, something nobody else has ever done. But his victory is temporary. He sprints away, seeking an exit from the Matrix (his Magic Flight). He has almost found it but walks right into the barrel of one of the agent's guns. The agent pumps half a dozen rounds into Neo's chest. Neo stumbles backward into a wall and slinks down, dying in the world of illusion. Trinity, his ally and symbol of divine feminine love, is watching in shock from the ship. In an act of hope and love, she kisses Neo (his real body is back on the ship). He begins to breathe again, and his vital signs return. He rises to face the agents who turn back in bewilderment. Now everything has changed once and for all. Neo has overcome death in the Matrix. He has reawakened to a new level of consciousness, and now it's the enemy who is on the run.

He Is Risen

After Jesus's death his Disciples go into hiding. They don't know if they will be next to hang on a cross. They are devastated, confused and fearful. The crucifixion of their leader has not been remotely close to the ending they had envisioned. They lock themselves up in a small room to mourn and work out what to do next. Three days after their world has come crashing down around them, Mary Magdalene shows up out of breath. She has just been to Jesus's tomb and has come to them to share her revelation. So excited she can barely get the words out, she tells the disciples that she has seen the risen Messiah. It's wishful thinking, they decide, and dismiss Mary's report as an imaginary vision of a distraught and grieving woman. Later that evening Jesus walks through the wall of the room that his Disciples are using as their hideout:

> *On the evening of that first day of the week, when the disciples were together, with the doors locked for fear of the Jewish leaders, Jesus came and stood among them and said, "Peace be with you!" After he said this, he showed them his hands and side. The disciples were overjoyed when they saw the Lord. Again Jesus said, "Peace be with you! As the Father has sent me, I am sending you."* (John 20:20-22 NIV)

The Atonement opens the door for all Heroes to approach the Father once again. When Jesus says "It is finished" in his last moments on the Cross, he means that he has dealt with sin once and for all. He has made the required sacrifice for all of his image-bearers to be readopted into the family of the Heavenly Father. In that fateful moment, we become co-heirs with Christ, and when we share in his sufferings (i.e. when we take up our own Cross), we also share in his glory. In his letter to the Romans, Paul states we are dead to sin thirty-eight different times. Jesus's death wiped the slate clean, but it also set up his next critical act: the Resurrection. When he appears to Mary Magdalene and then to his Disciples on that first Easter Sunday 2,000 years ago, he demonstrates that he has overcome not only sin but also death itself.

We think of death as the end, but Jesus reminds us that death is just part of the cycle of life. The story doesn't end when the Hero dies; the story gets better. In the words of Joseph Campbell, "The conquest of the fear of death is the recovery of life's joy. One can experience an unconditional affirmation of life only when one has accepted death, not as contrary to life but as an aspect of life. Life in its becoming is always shedding death, and on the point of death. The conquest of fear yields the courage of life. That is the cardinal initiation of every heroic adventure—fearlessness and achievement."[1]

The Truest Story Ever Told

I have titled this book *The Truest Story Ever Told* because the Word became Flesh and came down to live on this earth. And then the Word, Jesus, wrote his story as the archetype of the eternal life-renewing story in which we are all meant to share. That story operates on us on multiple levels. First, through the accounts of the Gospels, we can study the timeless wisdom of his life and teachings. Second, Jesus's story means our stories will not be written in vain. His death is our death. His Resurrection is ours, too. He conquered death, and we will enjoy it's eternal benefits. The fear of death may be laid to rest because it no longer indicates that the story is over. Death bears life. The Hero who wants to grow figures out how to die. He dies to all the ways he has tried to protect himself from being vulnerable. He lays his fears on the Cross. And when he loses his life, he finds it.

Still, Jesus' story operates on an even deeper level than the previous two because his story does more than inform and enable our own stories. At the most fundamental level, his story is our story. Consider this notion for a moment. Paul wrote, "I have been crucified with Christ and I no longer live, but Christ lives in me. The life I now live in the body, I live by faith in the Son of God, who love me and gave himself for me." (Gal. 2:20 NIV) When the Gospel of John refers to Jesus as the Word (or *Logos*), it means he is the cosmic order of the Universe. He is the source of life itself. The entire earth was created as a reflection of the Word, Jesus. When we come to live under his authority, we take on his life and that becomes in the spiritual-eternal sense the truest thing about us. His story is the *Truest Story Ever Told*, and we get to take part in it.

His cosmic personality is all around us and has never been far from the heart of man. The changing of seasons bears witness to his triumph. Every flower in spring gives testimony to the promise of resurrection—life, death and renewal in an eternal cycle. Without coordination the Hero's Journey has emerged in man's collective conscious, in his dreams and in his most sacred stories. But man was separated from the Word by the entrance of evil and sin. Throughout the ages man was reminded of the void but had no answers, so he wrote his myths hoping to discover the truth. Then Jesus, the Word, showed up and said, "I am the Truth." (John 14:6 NIV) He didn't come to replace the hope written in the hearts of man and chronicled in the stories of antiquity. He came to fulfill them.

Jesus's Resurrection began a new chapter. He confronted and defeated Death. By his willing participation in the trials and suffering of human life, Jesus ensured we would join in his eternal life. That eternal life begins upon acceptance of his gift, meaning we don't have to wait until we die to enjoy the fruits of his promise. Instead, eternity is upon us. The Word has come to take his residence within us. His spirit mixes with the Hero's spirit in this wondrous mystical way until, like the merging of two great rivers, it's unclear where he stops and we begin. And that is why we know his Hero story—because it is our story. Our life will be Jesus's life because he has come to dwell in us with the same cosmic order and spirit that existed before time. We will be resurrected, too. And until we meet that fateful day in the biological sense, we have the privilege of rehearsing it symbolically during our days on the earth. How? By making our own Hero's Journey with Jesus as our guide.

Reentry

For the past ten years, I have attended a week-long men's retreat in Colorado. The week is marked by adventure, community with other men and long periods of quiet reflection and prayer. For most men who attend, the week is a micro-cycle of the entire Hero's Journey. Often all of the steps we have discussed up to this point take place in a contracted period of time. My favorite event of the week is a drive by jeep over the Continental Divide. It takes two or three hours to traverse the rocky and rugged trails that wind through the aspen groves and then up above the tree line before cresting along a mountain pass 13,000 feet above sea level. We get out at the top and spend more than an hour there. It's twenty degrees cooler there than at the bottom of the mountain. The wind whips past us. The view is epic: a 360-degree panorama of the ancient Rockies. It feels like another planet among an endless sea of pointed peaks and domes jutting up through the clouds. An hour of silent prayer up there has a profound impact on all of us.

On the last night of the retreat, the leader always offers a warning about what to expect when we return to what we have labeled in this project as the "Ordinary World." How do we come down from a mountaintop "high" and return to work, family and all the e-mails awaiting our return? The leader warns us that reentry may not be comfortable. Our wife has been home all week by herself with sick kids. Our to-do list doesn't go away while we are riding in a jeep in Colorado; it is still there. The deadline we have at work is now a week closer. We have committed a week to deliberately work on ourselves. We should be commended for our effort, but the rest of the world doesn't care. It will expect the same things from us when we get home that it did when we left.

The challenge of the Hero's Journey is to integrate the mountaintop experiences into everyday existence. Our life doesn't take place at 13,000 feet. It takes place in the cities and suburbs. We work in office buildings and cubicles, in schools, restaurants and construction sites. We pay our taxes and health insurance premiums, visit the dentist and our car's mechanic, and run on conveyor belts for exercise. Resurrection into the Ordinary World comes in the way our spiritual accomplishments and discoveries manifest themselves in daily life. In other words, the Resurrection comes as a renewed perspective on our identity, and we don't share that new identity in certain contexts; we make that new identity known in all contexts of our life. Our transformation on the mountain filters its way into our careers, families, friendships and churches.

The reborn Hero is no longer a chameleon who always shifts identities to suit each situation and audience. He becomes more consistent and true no matter what the context is. He doesn't act one way with old high school friends and a different way with his small group from church. He doesn't swear like a sailor with one group of people but act more proper than Queen Elizabeth at high tea with another. He doesn't get around church people and suddenly try to work the words *blessed* and *the Lord* into every other sentence, but never uses the same language with coworkers. The Hero living from his true identity acts the same way regardless of who is watching. The mountaintop experience filters into all aspects of life. When the Hero's reentry into to the Ordinary World is secured by a renewed identity, he no longer has to continually compartmentalize life. He can be who he was born to be in all of his activities.

Another challenge of reentry into the Ordinary World is that not everyone will be excited by the changes wrought by our Hero's Journey. If we have always played a certain role and now begin to live more authentically, this new identity may disrupt the delicate balances in our relationships. We discussed Threshold Guardians at the outset of the Hero's Journey. Those same Guardians (e.g., bosses, parents, friends, spouses, pastoral leaders) may still be waiting for us when we return. They didn't want us to go on the journey in the first place. They may be no less relieved when we come back more secure in our identity and purpose. We will have to get comfortable with the idea that our transformation may raise the level of conflict in our lives for a period of time as the boundaries of relationships get shifted around and we don't respond to the people in our lives out of fear or a need to please.

Our newfound identity might also be met with skepticism. This is particularly true if we have tried other "self-improvement" quests but have always slipped back into the old routine after a few weeks. Our goal shouldn't entail trying to prove ourselves or selling our newfound perspective to anyone else. The Hero does not live by words; he lives by action. When the leader of the retreat in Colorado gives advice about reentry, he stresses the importance of not returning and making bold claims. "Minimize the amount of talking you do about all the ways you are going to change," he suggests, "and let your life speak for itself." The person who feels compelled to always talk about how much he is "transformed" is usually the first person to fall back to the old self when he is challenged.

The Resurrection of the Hero marks the beginning of his new life and the launching point of bringing the rewards he has won during the Hero's Journey back to the Ordinary World in order to benefit his community and fellow man. The Hero has much to share in the way his life impacts those around him. Reintegration is not always an easy transition, but the Hero can't complete the cycle without applying what he has learned in the special world into the ordinary parts of his life. He must learn to master both experiences, which is the next phase of the Hero's Journey.

Master of Two Worlds

Ultimately, the Hero will come to understand that the other dimension from which he returns and the ordinary experience of his life are actually not distinct from each other. What he has discovered in his journey is a fuller sense of reality—that the mystical dimension has always been there waiting to be integrated into his daily life. By losing his life, he has found it, and with that he has discovered a wisdom born of humility about how to balance the material world with the spiritual world and the inner life with the outer life. With this mastery of both worlds, he is free to pour into his community the wisdom, love and insights he gleaned during the Hero's Journey.

In this step the Hero achieves balance between the material and spiritual worlds. He understands the connection between his inner and outer world. By the end of *Star Wars*, Luke has discovered how to live with the Force: He is wise, calm and assured. He is the last hope for the Jedi Order and is in complete contrast to the ignorant and compulsive farm boy he was before his journey.

In *The Matrix* Neo illustrates his mastery of both worlds when he makes the following proclamation to the machines that have designed the Matrix:

> *I know you're out there. I can feel you now. I know that you're afraid. You're afraid of us. You're afraid of change. I don't know the future. I didn't come here to tell you how this is going to end. I came here to tell you how it's going to begin. I'm going to hang up this phone. And then I'm gonna show this people what you don't want them to see. I'm gonna show them the world. Without you. A world without rules and controls, without borders or boundaries. A world ... where anything is possible. Where we go from there is a choice I'll leave to you."*

After his Resurrection Jesus spends forty days with his Apostles and various witnesses. He continues to teach and prepare them for what is to come and to assure them that he is not a ghost or a spirit but is with them in the flesh. When it's time for him to ascend to the right hand of the Father, he leaves them with these instructions: "Do not leave Jerusalem, but wait for the gift my Father promised, which you have heard me speak about. For John baptized with water, but in a few days you will be baptized with the Holy Spirit." (Acts 1:5 NIV)

A few days later Jesus delivers on his promise:

> When the day of Pentecost came, they were all together in one place. Suddenly a sound like the blowing of a violent wind came from heaven and filled the whole house where they were sitting. They saw what seemed to be tongues of fire that separated and came to rest on each of them. All of them were filled with the Holy Spirit and began to speak in other tongues as the Spirit enabled them. (Acts 2 NIV)

A crowd of people gathers, not knowing what to make of this scene. Some start making fun of those who have received the Holy Spirit. That's when Peter, who had denied Jesus three times and went into hiding after his death, gets up and gives the first sermon of the new church. He speaks with such authority and clarity that three thousand people are baptized and saved that day. Not a bad start for a fisherman. Jesus arrives as the Master of Two Worlds. He sits at the right hand of the Father and through the work of the Holy Spirit, pours his heavenly authority and power into his Heroes on earth.

Sovereignty

Throughout his ministry Jesus preached about the Kingdom of God. In the Gospel of Matthew, Jesus mentions *kingdom* fifty-six different times. A kingdom is a proclamation about authority or sovereignty. It answers the question, "Who is in charge of this territory?" Jesus's successful quest asserts God's sovereignty once again over the world and his image-bearers in it. The Apostle Paul writes, "And having disarmed the powers and authorities, he made a public spectacle of them, triumphing over them by the Cross." (Col. 2:15 NIV) God is master of both worlds; he reigns in heaven and on earth.

Who are the powers and authorities who were disarmed according to Paul? They are called by a number of different names in the Bible: enemy, Satan, prince of demons, prince of the world, the deceiver of the whole world, the father of lies, the accuser, adversary and prince of the power of the air. Jesus dethroned this enemy and his emissaries—they no longer have any authority over those who place themselves under God's Kingdom authority. Those who accept the gift that Jesus offered on the Cross do not have to live under the cruel dictatorship of an enemy who rules based on fear, death and destruction.

This Kingdom authority which Jesus brought over the Ordinary World (earth) extends itself to the Hero living in it. The Spirit Jesus sent back after his final exit gives each of us the right to assert God's sovereignty over the little kingdoms he has put in our care on earth. They might include our family, our home, our business, our relationships and any other forum that falls under our influence and power. As we surrender these various areas to him, he empowers us to rule as he would, that is, to have his will be done on earth as it is in Heaven—bringing his Kingdom into reality throughout our life.

God's reestablishment of his authority has another important implication relative to the adversary he has come to dethrone. Unfortunately, the adversary has not been completely eliminated. He prowls around like a roaring lion, seeking someone to devour. He is still stoking rebellion, and if he isn't trying to undermine us directly, he is coming after our spouse, our children, our friends and our coworkers. He is prowling around, even in our Ordinary World, trying to convince anyone he can to step outside God's Kingdom authority so that he can pounce and use what power he has left to undermine God's Heroes.

As Master of Two Worlds, the Hero is prepared to deal with this adversary. He addresses him as Neo addresses the machines that rule the Matrix in the quote above, which also reminds me of the advice given by James, Jesus's brother,: "Yell a loud no to the devil and watch him scamper." (James 4:6 NIV). When it comes to an enemy, most people are living in the Matrix. We aren't even aware of the enemy's presence because he isn't immediately available to our limited sensory experience. And, like Neo, until the end when he sees the entire truth, we remain unaware we have been given all the power and authority we need to defeat the adversary. That is why Christians pray in the name of Jesus—to ensure that the spiritual dimension understands whose banner we are carrying into battle. But those emissaries who want to corrupt and destroy all we love are afraid. They are afraid that we will recognize them and that we will clothe ourselves with the power and authority of Heaven and hurl them out of our area of dominion on earth.

The Hero who has made it this far learns to bring the sovereignty of Heaven to his Ordinary World. He must remain vigilant, but he no longer has to fear the prince of the world just as he no longer has to fear death because the Hero is no longer under the adversary's authority and rule. The prince of the world is on the run.

Passing Back and Forth

As Master of Two Worlds, the Hero doesn't have to ride a jeep to 13,000 feet to find spiritual sustenance. He doesn't have to go to church to get closer to God. He realizes the Mystical World and the Ordinary World are one, and he finds evidence of the Father's presence all around. Every morning is a chance for worship, and every conversation is an opportunity to reflect the Father's love back to the world. The Hero passes back and forth effortlessly between the two worlds. He no longer sees heaven and earth as disparate worlds. The quality of his life and love give testimony that heaven and earth have met.

The Hero's Journey helps us to walk in step with the Spirit that makes this all possible. Through a relationship with Jesus and following his lead into this great unknown, we are finally capable of doing that which we were incapable of doing on our own. Jesus has dealt with our sin once and for all. We share in his glory and righteousness by faith. His joy and peace are ours if we want them. The victory over Satan is won when we put on his armor and wield the sword of his Spirit.

The Hero who has discovered how to knit the Ordinary World with the special realm of the Spirit sees the quality of his life transformed. The mastery of two worlds means that we can receive the gifts Paul described like fruit in an orchard—"things like affection for others, exuberance about life, serenity. We develop a willingness to stick with things, a sense of compassion in the heart, and a conviction that a basic holiness permeates things and people. We find ourselves involved in loyal commitments, not needing to force our way in life, able to marshal and direct our energies wisely." (Gal. 5:22-23 MSG) Living this way doesn't come about through striving. This fruit isn't earned through the will; it's received as a gift. It's what results when we submit our lives to the *Truest Story Ever Told* and allow Jesus to remake us into the Heroes we were meant to be from the moment we were created.

CHAPTER XIII

FREEDOM TO LIVE

The Hero's mastery of both worlds also frees him from the fear of death, which in turn gives him the freedom to live. He is no longer anxious because his identity no longer finds its locus around his actions and deeds. Instead, he turns to the source of life itself and on his knees offers the fruit of those deeds as a living sacrifice. Time—the past and the future—is no longer his bondage, and so he lives fully present to all of creation in the knowledge that death will be defeated. His own ego has been subjugated, which gives him a greater capacity to love his fellow man and all of the world.

THE FORCE IN *STAR WARS* REPRESENTS an energy field created by all living things, binding the universe together. The Jedi have mastered the Force by willing submission to it. Fear has no power over the Jedi, and because of it they live as a royal priesthood, giving their lives in sacrifice to protect the universe from those enemies who would use the Force to satisfy their own egos. In *Return of the Jedi,* Luke shows his Freedom to Live when he refuses to align himself with the dark side by casting aside his lightsaber instead of using it to kill his father. He no longer fears death. To Luke death remains a better alternative to perpetuating the anger, fear and violence that came to characterize his father's existence. He trusts the Force is greater than death itself.

In the closing scene of *The Wizard of Oz,* Dorothy wakes up to see her family and friends gathered around her. She tries to tell them about Oz but is overwhelmed by being home. She proclaims that she will never leave them again because she loves them too much, and the movie closes with Dorothy saying, "Oh Auntie Em, there's no place like home." But home is not just meant literally. Dorothy is finally home in her own soul, and that has freed her to live fully in the Ordinary World, to feel at home in her identity and to freely love her family and friends instead of feeling isolated and conflicted the way she did before her journey through Oz began.

We are told that Jesus completed his journey when he was taken up to heaven and seated at the right hand of the Father. Then God "put all things under his feet (Jesus) and gave him as head over all things to the church, which is his body, the fullness of him who fills all in all." (Eph. 1:20-23 ESV). Jesus now sits on his eternal throne, pouring his love out into the world through his loyal heroes. By embracing death and taking it upon himself, he has defeated it on our behalf. We no longer have to cower through life in fear. Death and sin have been replaced by love and forgiveness. He reigns from heaven over all of the world, freeing us, should we turn to him, to live fully present in our lives and no longer captive to the flesh or our enemies.

An End with a Twist

When we think about the genre of the Hero's Journey up to this point, we might be apt to label it an adventure story, an action thriller or a drama. It is all of these things, but at its core the Hero's Journey is a love story. It's about the quintessential Hero coming to earth and making a journey we can all follow. He makes the journey out of love, with us as the object. He comes to give us sight, to free us from our prison and to bind up our broken hearts. For God so loved the world that he sent his son to rescue his image-bearers. Therefore, the final phase of the Hero's Journey, The Freedom to Live, is also the Freedom to Love.

Through our travels as Heroes, we learn to subvert the ego. We lay to rest those old identities and awaken to a higher state of consciousness, no longer enslaved by the ego's self-protective mechanisms and unquenchable need to assert its importance. Instead, we find the freedom to live true. And when a Hero lives true with an awareness that he no longer must fear death (real or symbolic), his greatest reward is that he transcends all the ways in which his previous life and identity have held him back. The Hero comes to understand the paradox that in order for him to find his deepest center, he must pass entirely out of himself and pour himself out in pure sacrificial love to other people.

In that state of transcendence, he receives into his innermost being the love that has existed since the beginning of time. He understands that the closest thing he can get to the personality and nature of God, which defies any human conception imaginable, is love. Or as John reminds us in his letter, "And so we know and rely on the love God has for us. God is love. Whoever lives in love lives in God, and God in them." (1 John 4:16 NIV) And because the Hero is no longer concerned for his ego, he can take the step required to experience the depth and width of that love. As he has abandoned his former and limited self-conceptions, he becomes intertwined with God and he too becomes love. He doesn't have to strive as hard to love his neighbor as himself. He just does. He loves because he is loved.

Image Bearing

At the conclusion of Part I of this book, I suggested that our mission is to bear God's image on earth. But how do we go about bearing the image of a creator who makes the stars his footstool, has conceived of a world as beautiful, detailed and diverse as earth and lives within and beyond time? The best approximation we can come up with of him is love. His nature is relational. If we want to understand who he is, love is the best clue. If we want to reflect him, love is our calling. Trappist monk and author Thomas Merton wrote, "To say that I am made in the image of God is to say that love is the reason for my existence, for God is Love. Love is my true identity. Selflessness is my true self. Love is my true character. Love is my name." [1]

The outcome of our Hero's Journey is that our capacity to love grows. We become clearer reflections of God's intended purpose because our life overflows with his love. The Hero's Journey frees us from the central burden that prevents us from loving well: the fear of our vulnerability. C. S. Lewis wrote, "To love is to be vulnerable."[2] Until the fear of being alone or of feeling insignificant or exposed are laid to rest, we will not experience the freedom to be truly vulnerable. Lewis continues this train of thought: ... "Love anything and your heart will be wrung and possibly broken. If you want to make sure of keeping it intact you must give it to no one, not even an animal. Wrap it carefully round with hobbies and little luxuries; avoid all entanglements. Lock it up safe in the casket or coffin of your selfishness. But in that casket, safe, dark, motionless, airless, it will change. It will not be broken; it will become unbreakable, impenetrable, irredeemable."[3]

When we successfully venture into the Hero's Journey, two essential things are accomplished that free us to love wholeheartedly. First, in order for us to pour out love, we must receive it. If we don't believe we are loved and accepted, we won't have the capacity to share love and acceptance with others. If we bear our vulnerability and get rejected, it affirms the message that we are alone, insignificant or exposed, resulting in our shutting down our heart to protect it from further pain. This limits how much of ourselves we can give to others, just as Lewis suggests above. It caps our love at the edge of our vulnerability. Or, said another way, our love is conditional.

The only solution is to find our primary source of love from a place other than the people we have sought love from most of our lives. The reason we can't be 100 percent vulnerable is because the people who raised us and everyone else with whom we have come in contact are dealing with the same things. They are also Adam or Eve hiding in the forest, covering themselves with fig leaves. So they have their own limitations, and that is why we hurt each other. We have all been hurt at some point by those to whom we have looked most for love. In fact, hurt might be a gross understatement for the pain many of us have experienced. The shortcomings of our closest relationships may be a source of tremendous pain and disappointment.

Before we can move on and change the narrative about love in our lives, we have to turn to the source of perfect love, God the Father. This is why the Atonement is the central step in our transformation as Heroes. We learn that the Father can be trusted, and if we will take the time to listen and seek his words for our lives, he will show us his character. And we now know that character is love. It's not love in the sense we may have known in our human relationships. With the Father we experience love in its unconditional and sacrificial purity. And when we understand that the creator of life loves us unconditionally and sacrificially, then we realize that all the ways in which we feared we have been lacking don't matter. The highest expression of life itself, Jesus, has said that we're good enough, worthy and beloved because we just are. He tells us to stop striving to earn everyone else's love and to stop striving to earn his. The story has already been written, and it's a love story. There is nothing we can do to change it. The only choice we have is whether or not to believe it.

The Cross is the highest symbol of life because it is God's symbolic act for displaying his love to mankind. On the Cross he makes love personal. He shows us what it is like at a tangible and agonizingly human level, demonstrating the level of sacrifice he is willing to make for us. Theologian Hans ur Von Balthasar says the gift is "too beautiful to be true" and the measures taken for us are incomprehensible:

The mystery of being, unveiled as absolute love, coming down to wash the feet and the souls of its creatures; a love that assumes the whole burden of our guilt and hate, that accepts the accusations that shower down, the disbelief that veils God again when he has revealed himself, all the scorn and contempt that nails down his incomprehensible movement of self-abasement—all this, absolute love accepts in order to excuse his creature before himself and before the world. [4]

After we come to accept the great love of God in our life, then we are free to share that love with the world. Joseph Campbell said the Hero's Journey is an endless cycle. "The only way to close it is to return with something the Hero didn't have and share it with his fellow man."[5] The best thing we can share is ourselves. We can pour out our life for others. God's love for us frees us to give away the best we have, our first-fruits, just as he did on the Cross.

Therefore, we bear his image by how well we love. If you want the Cliff Notes version of what Jesus taught in his three years of ministry it is this: "This is My commandment, that you love one another as I have loved you." (John 15:12 NIV) This is the only time in Jesus's ministry he ever proclaims, "This is My commandment." Jesus taught many incredible lessons and gave the world many great parables to ponder. But if we are to remember nothing else about how he wanted us to conduct our lives, he wants us to remember to love well.

When we love well, it begins with God and moves out in concentric circles through the world of our relationships. Those closest to us, our families, are the barometer for how we are doing. They are the ones who live with us through good days and bad. They see our true colors, and if we are in a position to love well, they should, by their proximity, be the first to benefit. They are also the first ones to suffer when we aren't loving well. We can get involved in ministry and justice missions, but we don't have to leave home to see how things are really going with our love. In his book, Promise Keepers founder Bill

McCartney relays a story about a message he heard that made him reconsider how he was doing relationally. The speaker said to him, "When you look into the face of a man's wife, you will see just what he is as a man. Whatever he has invested in or withheld from her is reflected in her countenance."[6] McCartney explains that when he turned to look at his wife, he saw a tired woman who had given everything to her husband's career while receiving little in return. We live with the product of how we love, and when we love well, the people around us flourish. When we don't love well, we wear down those closest to us and it slowly drains the life out of them.

One of the benefits of loving others well is that we realize we don't have to carry the burden of fixing them. We don't have the responsibility of fixing anyone else either, nor do we have the power to begin with. That is a job we leave to the Father. Instead of spending our energies trying to organize the redemption and salvation of others, we focus our efforts on simply loving them. We can meet people right where they are and love them in spite of their brokenness. By our love, grace and acceptance, we can point them beyond us toward the perfecting love that their Heavenly Father would like to pour out on their lives.

No wife wants to be "fixed" by her husband. Friends don't develop deep bonds because one party uses the relationship to get the other party in line. Children eventually rebel against parents who focus on control at the expense of unconditional love. The world doesn't need more fixers, controllers and armchair psychologists. It needs more examples of compassion, kindness, forgiveness and empathy. My dad always says, "People don't care how much you know, until they know how much you care." But we tend to start with advice and "I told you so" when people we know struggle. While there is something to being able to speak truth and wisdom in someone's life, the authority to do so comes out of love. The advice resonates when the person already knows how much we care and that our motive is love instead of the satisfaction of being right or getting recognition for notching another "saved soul" on our belt.

Loving well is not really complicated. We see a need, and we meet it, with no expectation of anything in return and not because it benefits us. We show up. We make dinner. We get on a plane. We throw a party. We drop everything on a moment's notice. We call out of the blue. We give up our money, our vacation and our free time. We do whatever love asks.

In the buzz of life, recognition of a need is far from a given for most of us. When we live in our small little stories with the world revolving around our problems and cares, it's easy to miss the important cues about what is going on that matters. We miss opportunities to fill a need because we are going too fast or are too self-involved to notice. But the Hero has been freed from the pace of life everyone else seems to think is normal, and he sees his story as part of an epic tale about God and his love for this world. The Hero shows up because he notices.

What a lot of us label as "love-ing" acts are secretly about us. We might do something sweet for our wife, but we are hoping she will return the favor later. Often, we do things out of fear. Our motive for meeting a need is to avoid conflict or disappointment from the other person. Sometimes recognition drives us. We do loving things because it's part of our identity. We are pleasers, but deep down, if we are honest, our love has a selfish aim; it's a manipulation of the way we want to be perceived.

Loving others well means we sacrifice for them without getting upset when they don't do likewise for us. It means we do things without secret agendas. We love as Jesus did because "greater love has no one than this, that he lay down his life for his friends." (John 15:13 NIV) When we lay down our life, we are putting our identity on the line. We are dying to how we have protected ourselves and organized the world to puff ourselves up. It's difficult to avoid keeping an invisible ledger in our head about who owes who what. But love doesn't keep a ledger. Who is winning isn't under consideration when we recognize the joy of allowing the love poured out for us by our Heavenly Father to spill out into our relationships.

Coming Full Circle

This quest doesn't end with an answer; it ends with another question—"What is next?" We never complete the Hero's Journey. We are forever in process. St. Augustine talked about not *being* a "Christian" but always becoming a Christian. Blaise Pascal believed true Christianity involved a continual remaking of oneself in the image and spirit of Jesus (*imitatio Christi*). When God appeared to Moses in the Old Testament, he said my name is "I am that I am." (Ex 3:14 NIV) He is always *becoming*. There is no static ending point. All Heroes are also becoming. They are in process, always rehearsing and practicing their eternal roles.

Every Hero's Journey has its own fingerprint. There is no rigid formula, only an important framework for contemplating the context of our lives and an idea of how we might live more richly. Since the dawn of time, man has been dreaming about Heroes and sharing those stories through the timeless stories we call myths. Then a man showed up in history, and another mythical Hero story was told, but this time it was real. It was the *Truest Story Ever Told*, and he is a miracle because he is both myth and fact. Now the author of life is inviting you, no matter how ordinary your station, to come take part in the mythical wonder of it all, to take up your part in the epic story of creation.

The God of the Universe put you hear for a reason. It wasn't to make sure your e-mail in-box is empty at the end of each day. In the Psalms it says:

> When I consider your heavens, the work of your fingers, the moon and the stars, which you have set in place, what is mankind that you are mindful of them, human beings that you care for them? You have made them a little lower than the angels and crowned them with glory and honor.
> You made them rulers over the works of your hands; you put everything under their feet: all flocks and herds
> and the animals of the wild,
> the birds in the sky,
> and the fish in the sea,
> all that swim the paths of the seas
> (Ps. 8:3-6 NIV)

You're more than a cosmic accident. Sin no longer rules. You may become a Hero if you choose to be. Your life can be fused with the life of the Hero of all Heroes and crowned with glory and honor. The question is, "Are you ready for your destiny?

CHAPTER XIV

STARTING YOUR STORY

BECAUSE WE ARE SUCH STORIED CREATURES, we live by them without even being aware of it. Stories are like the computer operating system of our lives. They run in the background, mostly invisible, powering all of the other applications we need to operate in this world. They create the framework for our decisions, relationships and aspirations.

If you want to make important and lasting changes in your life, tell yourself a better story. If you want to help others, help them improve their stories. If you want to change the culture of your workplace, school, church or community, change the stories people tell themselves about those things.

That is what the Hero's Journey offers—a different way to interpret the events of our life. It takes what sometimes might seem random and unconnected events and circumstances and places them into a coherent narrative. It gives us a story that inspires hope. That is what I hope to have accomplished with this book: to convince the intellect that the stories it has been telling itself often have been inaccurate and to offer a better alternative. There is a reasonable and repeatable story sequence the intellect should be considering in its analysis of what's happening in each of our lives.

We tell ourselves a story when our career gets derailed. We tell ourselves a story when a relationship falls short of our expectations. We have origin stories about where we come from and what that means about who we will be going forward. Every success in life comes with a story as well. Our inability to live without stories means that they infiltrate every part of our lives, and the nature of the stories we believe to be true will determine how we respond in good times and bad. We can change our own lives and our communities by living from a better narrative than the one that is commonly offered. The Truest Story Ever Told changes everything. It becomes the truest part of your story, too, and the invitation awaits you to take your part in it.

Some Practical Advice

Before I conclude this book, I would like to offer a few practical suggestions before you set out on your Hero's Journey. We have been describing modern ordinary life in mythical terms. While that may be inspiring, it may also, at first, prove difficult to connect the phases of the Hero's special world with day-to-day life. The good news is you don't have to have all the answers to get started. It doesn't all have to make sense right now. With that in mind, the following areas are things you might consider to get you started.

Seek the Father's Voice

The Hero's Journey ends and begins from the same place—in love. Until you find security in love, finding the right adventure or summing up the courage to pursue it will be difficult. You may have your doubts about the authenticity of the Heavenly Father's love, which was discussed in the last chapter. You may have thoughts like, "He might love Mike, but he doesn't love me"; or "I am not sure he could love me after what I have done"; or "If he loved me, why do these bad things happen to me?"; or "I don't know if God would care about my little story" or "I don't know if I believe God is involved in my life at all." So before you set out on your adventure, I invite you to suspend all of your doubts, for a week, a month or some period of time, about God's love for you. Don't worry, you can always go back to whatever perspective you want. But just take a risk and assume you know nothing and that it is possible for some truths to go beyond what science and sensory experience can account for.

Once you have freed your mind from all of the limits it wants to put on God's love and participation in your life, find time to contemplate the Cross and Jesus. Or, if a particular passage of scripture comes to mind, contemplate that. Then, after a period of time meditating over this (there is no rigid prescription on length, timing or place), simply ask God to show you his love for you. Then listen to the still small voice in your heart. Stay there for a while; linger. When you feel enough time has elapsed, write any words or impressions you experienced.

Don't put any pressure on this activity. Just relax and open your heart to the possibility that the Spirit of Jesus wants to be an active participant in your life. Repeat the same thing the next day or the day after. Keep asking God to show you his love for you. Write whatever surfaces and go back and read it later. Eventually, you might begin to believe it, and when you do, you will find your next Hero's Journey becoming clearer. The risk might still send your heart racing, but you will have a little extra courage and motivation to get started. After all, you have the quintessential Hero at your side, and you will know his love is real.

Choose Your Measuring Device

The Hero who journeys out to the frontier is operating beyond the protection of society. He is no longer measured by the standards of the community. People don't know what to make of him because all of the ways society has come up with to assign value to people and things seem to be lost on him. He has joined a small band of people who will not content themselves with the values and assumptions of popular opinion. The Hero's work is creative, pushing at the fringes of his community to establish a new set of norms and expectations for what it means to live a good life.

So, as you consider the adventures that may call you, it is helpful to decide what you will use as your measuring device. Society demands that we measure our lives by money, status in various social groups, appearances and making it to the top of the podium in an endeavor that the people in our community deem meaningful. There is tremendous pressure to measure your life by these type of standards. Before you set out, decide what you want, how you will evaluate whether you are headed in the right direction and what is the North

Star by which you will set your compass. Your choice about what measuring stick you will live by will determine the missions you choose and your willingness to stick with them when things get difficult.

This isn't a goal-setting exercise or another way to create pressure to perform. It's choosing what you value. If you don't live with clarity about the values, relationships and activities that drive you, you will get sucked into the vortex of what society values. Without even knowing it, your hopes and desires will shift toward following what the culture values. You will unknowingly buy into the lies that life and happiness are just around the corner if only you can improve your status in the areas society deems important.

How you spend your money, time and your emotional and mental energy reveal more than anything else about how you are trying to measure your life. If you say your relationship with your children is important but you work eighty hours a week and travel all the time, then what you are saying is important doesn't match what you really believe is important. Your measuring stick isn't a great relationship with your children, even though you might have convinced yourself otherwise. It's some achievement at work or attainment of a certain level of monetary status. It's easy to fall into this trap, stating one set of priorities because it sounds good but operating from a completely different set of priorities in your life.

Here is a thought experiment you can repeat that might bring clarity to how you measure yourself. Take a blank piece of paper and draw a table with two columns and three rows. Take some time for reflection, and in each of the rows in the first column, write down your answer to the following:

Row 1: How do you want to prioritize your relationships?
Row 2: How do you want other people to perceive you?
Row 3: What character values are most important to you?

Think of your answers in aspirational terms. Who is it you want to be in these three areas?

After you have written down your answers, take a couple of weeks or so and pretend you have another person (a "life auditor") following you around and auditing every second of your life. Imagine that person riding with you every time you get in the car, sitting with you at every meal, listening in on every phone conversation, analyzing your bank account and credit card statements, chronicling the website and social media accounts you visit online. The imaginary auditor tracks every detail of your life for two weeks. Pretend at the conclusion of the monitoring period that you receive a report on your life in the three areas identified above. The report provides an objective third-party summary based on careful observation of your daily life. In the second column, write down in each corresponding row how a life auditor would answer those questions about you after spending two weeks shadowing your every move.

This is a difficult exercise because it requires objective self-analysis. (A spouse might be helpful if he or she has the freedom to give you objective feedback in sensitive areas). However, if you can be honest with yourself, you might be surprised when you write what a third party would conclude about your life after careful analysis. This isn't an exercise that should make you feel discouraged. There is a gap between who all of us want to be and who we really are. The goal of the Hero's Journey is to close that gap. This is a practical way to begin to identify and measure the gaps for yourself. Each area of your life where there is a gap might serve as your next Call to Adventure, the next place you might grow and mature as a Hero.

This self-reflection might also reveal the ways you have internalized the measuring sticks you have chosen for your life and alert you to areas in which you are living to measure up without even realizing it. You can live by a different set of measures than the ones pushed on you by your family, friends and the culture. But first you have to grow in awareness of where your system of measurement has been hijacked.

Follow Desire

Lastly, begin to follow your desire. Take notice when you feel most alive or when you lose track of time because you are so engaged and present in whatever it is you are doing. Pay attention to what moves you emotionally or inspires you. Ask yourself what lights you up.

What would you do if money and time were not an issue? What makes you feel like Erik Liddell when he ran; when you do it, you feel God's pleasure?

Try to determine what makes you feel whole, a little more alive, a little more fulfilled, and then take a step. Stop thinking and do it. It's not about getting everything right or making sure every detail is accounted for; it's about starting. Just take a step and then get up the next day and take another one. Don't focus on the destination. Focus on the journey. When I started to write this book, the prospect of a finished product was far too daunting. So I decided I would write 500 words a day, good or bad (and many days they were bad). I would get up, and I would move. I wouldn't worry too much about when I would be finished or what it would all look like in the end. I just got up, and I wrote in the moment. For five months I did this. I tried not to overthink it. Five hundred words at a time I wrote until one day I was here, in the final pages. You can do the same thing in whatever is calling you.

The only thing holding you back from answering your Call to Adventure is you. You don't have to be the victim of your own life. Looking around for someone else to blame for your circumstances, for your pain and for your disappointment will only keep you stuck where you are. You have a choice now—there is an endless world of possibilities out there waiting for you. You can say no to fear. You can tell the Threshold Guardians you no longer accept their plan for your life. You don't have to wait until the path and outcomes are all clear, because they will never be clear; otherwise, it wouldn't be a journey worth taking.

Now it's your turn. The next chapter is yours to write. So, get started. And remember, God created man because God loves stories.

POSTSCRIPT

Thank you for making this journey with me through this book. I would love to hear about the Hero's Journey you are making. Please reach out to me at meddy@thewholehearted.org

Also, check out our website at www.thewholehearted.org to keep up with other projects we are working on.

NOTES

Chapter I

1. Fritz Heider and Marianne Simmel, The American Journal of Psychology Vol. 57, No. 2 (Apr., 1944), pp. 243-259

2. https://www.youtube.com/watch?v=wp8ebj_yRI4

3. University of Colorado Denver. "Early human burials varied widely but most were simple. ScienceDaily. ScienceDaily, 21 February 2013.

4. New Yorker Magazine, Judith Thurman. "What does the world's oldest art say about us." (June 23, 2008).

5. Bertman, Stephen. *Handbook of Life in Ancient Mesopotamia.* Oxford University Press, 2003. Print.

6. New Yorker Magazine, Judith Thurman. "What does the world's oldest art say about us." (June 23, 2008).

7. Ibid

8. Gottschall, Jonathan. *Storytelling Animal.* Houghton Mifflin Harcourt Publishing Company, 2013. Kindle Edition.

9. Ibid

10. Pinker, Stephen. *The Language Instinct: The New Science of Language and Mind.* Harper Collins, 1994. Kindle Edition.

11. Chomsky, Noam. *Language and Mind.* Cambridge University Press, 2006. Print.

12. Deacon, Terrence W.. *The Symbolic Species: The Co-evolution of Language and the Brain.* W. W. Norton & Company. Kindle Edition.

13. Barfield Owen. *Poetic Diction.* London: Wesleyan University Press, 1973. Ebook edition. Barfield is quoting Ralph Waldo Emerson.

14. Wiesel, Elie. *Gates of the Forest.* Behrman House, 1994. Printed Edition.

15. Koblin, John. "How Much Do We Love TV? Let us Count the Ways." *nytimes.com.* New York Times, 30 June 2016. Web. 12 Jan 2018.

16. Gottschall, Jonathan. *Storytelling Animal.* Houghton Mifflin Harcourt Publishing Company, 2013. Kindle Edition.

17. Ibid

18. Armstrong, Karen. *A Short History of Myth.* New York: Canongate Books, 2005. Print.

Chapter II

1. Seabrook, John. "WHY IS THE FORCE STILL WITH US." newyorker.com. The New Yorker. 6 Jan. 1997. Web. 25 Jan 2018.

2. "Star Wars." Website. Boxofficemojo.com.

3. https://www.youtube.com/watch?v=bSyyqctan2c This is a clip from an award dinner featuring George Lucas with Joseph Campbell.

4. Densham, Pen. *Riding the Alligator: Strategies for a Career in Screenplay Writing and Not getting Eaten.* Studio City: Michael Wiese Productions, 2011. Print.

5. Campbell, Joseph. *Hero with a Thousand Faces.* New York: MJF Books, 1949. Print.

6. Ibid

7. Lewis, C.S.. *Miracles.* New York: HarperOne, 1996. 218. Print

Chapter III

1. Woodford, Chris. "A brief history of computers." *explainthatstuff.com* 7 Dec. 2017. Web. 10 Feb. 2018.

2. Ferry, Luc. A Brief History of Thought: *A Philosophical Guide to Living.* New York: HarperCollins Publishers, 2011. 127. Kindle Edition.

3. Ibid

4. Ibid

5. Descartes, René. *Rules for the Direction of the Mind.* Works of the Public Domain. Print Edition.

6. Jerphagnon, Lucien and Orcibal, Jean. "Blaise Pascal." *Encylopaedia Britanica.* 2018. Web.

7. "Blaise Pascal Scientific and spiritual prodigy." *christianitytoday.com.* Christianity Today. Web.

8. Buxton, Richard G. *From myth to reason?: studies in the development of Greek thought.* Oxford: Oxford Univ. Press, 2005. Print.

9. Ibid

10. Campbell, Joseph and Moyers, Bill. *The Power of Myth.* Anchors Books 1988. The Power of Myth is a compilation of a series of interviews journalist Bill Moyers conducted with Joseph Campbell for PBS in the 1980s. Many segments of the original interviews can be found online.

11. Menzies, James W.. *True Myth: C. S. Lewis and Joseph Campbell on the Veracity of Christianity* (38-39). Pickwick Publications, an Imprint of Wipf and Stock Publishers. Kindle Edition.

12. Skeel, David. *True Paradox: How Christianity Makes Sense of Our Complex World* (86). Downers Grove: InterVarsity Press, 2014. Kindle Edition.

13. "Karen Armstrong Builds a 'Case for God.'" *Author Interviews.* NPR. 21 Sept. 2009. Radio

14. Chesterton, GK. *Orthodoxy.* Works of the Public Domain. Kindle Edition.

Chapter IV

1. Lewis, CS. *Surprised by Joy.* HarperOne, 1995. Kindle Edition

2. Ibid

3. Lewis, CS "Myth became Fact," *God in the Dock.* William Eerdmans Publishing Company, 1970. Kindle Edition. CS Lewis wrote numerous essays during his career. *God in the Dock* is a compilation of some of his work including the essay quoted here.

4. Lewis, CS "Religion without Dogma," *God in the Dock*. William Eerdmans Publishing Company, 1970. Kindle Edition.

5. Chesterton, GK. *Everlasting Man*. Wilder Publications. Kindle Edition.

6. Ibid

7. Clement of Alexandria, *Miscellanies* 6.8 (PG. 9. 288), Migne, Patrologia, vol. 9, col. 288

8. Augustine of Hippo, *The Retractations*, ed. Roy Joseph Deferrari, trans. Mary Inez Bogan, vol. 60, The Fathers of the Church (Washington, DC: The Catholic University of America Press, 1968), 52.

9. Campbell, Joseph and Moyers, Bill. *The Power of Myth*. Anchors Books 1988. The Power of Myth is a compilation of a series of interviews journalist Bill Moyers conducted with Joseph Campbell for PBS in the 1980s. Many segments of the original interviews can be found online.

Chapter V

1. Willard, Dallas. *Divine Conspiracy*. New York: HarperCollins. Kindle.

2. Armstrong, Karen. *The Case for God*. New York: Anchor Books, 2009. Print.

3. Ehrman, Bart. *Forged*. New York: HarperCollins, 2011. Print.

4. Turner, Ryan. "An Analysis of the Pre-Pauline Creed in 1 Corinthians 15:1-11." *CARM.org*. Christian Apologetics and Research Ministry. This is a well cited and detailed article documenting the likely timeline, source(s) and place Paul received the Creed he relayed to the Church in Corinth.

5. Wright NT. *The Day The Revolution Began: Reconsidering the Meaning of Jesus' Crucifixion*. HarperOne, 2016. Digital Edition. I relied heavily on Wright's overview of the historical context of Jesus life and the likely perspectives of 1st century Jews in this section of the book.

6. Hackett, Conrad and MCClendon, David. "Christians remain world's largest religious group, but they are declining in Europe." *pewresearch.org.* Pew Research Center. 5 April 2017. Web. 3 March 2018.

7. "Why Missions." WorldHopperMinistry.com. World Hopper Ministry.

8. Wright NT. *The Day The Revolution Began: Reconsidering the Meaning of Jesus' Crucifixion.* HarperOne, 2016. Digital Edition.

Chapter VI

1. Luther, King M. Jr. "A Letter from Birmingham Jail." Published August 1963.

2. Ibid

3. Wright NT. *The Day The Revolution Began: Reconsidering the Meaning of Jesus' Crucifixion.* HarperOne, 2016. Digital Edition.

4. Ibid

5. Willard, Dallas. *Divine Conspiracy.* New York: HarperCollins. Kindle.

6. Lewis, CS. *Screwtape Letters.* New York: HarperCollins, 2001. Print.

7. Willard, Dallas. *Divine Conspiracy.* New York: HarperCollins. Kindle.

8. Brooks, David. *Road to Character.* New York: Random House, 2015. Kindle.

Chapter VII

1. Campbell, Joseph and Moyers, Bill. *The Power of Myth.* Anchors Books 1988. This comes from an interview of Campbell by journalist Bill Moyers.

Chapter VIII

1. Ferguson, Sinclair. *The Holy Spirit.* (p.100) Downers Grove: InterVarsity Press, 1996

2. Idid (p.56)

3. Balthasar, Hans ur von. *Love Alone is Credible.* (p.10) Ignatius Press, 2004

Chapter IX

1. This paragraph is my summary of Matthew 4. Campbell offers a similar kind of summary in his interview with Moyers in *Power of Myth.*

2. Edison reportedly said this in response to a New York times interviewer but I could not find the original source.

3. Gillett, Rachel. "From welfare to on of the wealthiest women: the incredible rags-to-riches story of J.K. Rowling." *businessinsider.com* Business Insider. 18 May 2015. Web. 10 May 2018.

4. Medeiros, Jenny. "Walt Disney's Life Story: A Mouse, Eternal Life, and a Stolen Rabit." *GoalCast.com.* 17 Jan. 2018 Web. 10 May 2018.

5. Campbell, Joseph and Moyers, Bill. *The Power of Myth.* Anchors Books 1988.

6. Gladwell, Malcolm. *David and Goliath: Underdogs, Misfits, and the Art of Battling Giants.* Little, Brown and Company. Kindle Edition.

7. Eldredge, John. *Wild at Heart.* Nashville: Thomas Nelson, 2001.

Chapter X

1. See *Strong's Concordance* for the Greek word *psychen*

2. Brown, Brene. *Daring Greatly.* New York: Penguin Random House, 2012.

3. Pascal, Blaise. *Thoughts.* Translated by Trotter, W. F. New York: Collier and Son, 1910. Print.

4. Jung, C.G. *Psychology and Alchemy.* New York: Bollingen, 1980. Print.

5. Lewis, CS. *The Voyage of the Dawn Treader.* New York: HarperCollins, 1952. Print.

6. Campbell, Joseph and Moyers, Bill. *The Power of Myth.* Anchors Books 1988.

Chapter XI

1. Lynch, John and McNicol, Bruce and Thrall, Bill. *The Cure.* San Clemente: CrossSection 2011. Kindle.

2. Frankl, Viktor E. *Man's Search for Meaning.* Boston: Beacon Press, 2006. Kindle.

3. Lewis, CS. *The Weight of Glory.* New York: HarperCollins, 1980. Kindle.

4. In his bestselling book, *Wild at Heart,* John Eldredge writes that this is the question that haunts every man; "Do I have what it takes?"

Chapter XII

1. Campbell, Joseph and Moyers, Bill. *The Power of Myth.* Anchors Books 1988. Kindle.

Chapter XIII

1. Merton, Thomas. *New Seeds of Contemplation.* New York: New Direction Books, 2007. Kindle.

2. Lewis, CS. *Four Loves.* New York: Harcourt, 1988. Print.

3. Ibid

4. Balthasar, Hans ur von. *Love Alone is Credible.* Ignatius Press, 2004. Kindle.

5. Campbell, Joseph and Moyers, Bill. *The Power of Myth.* Anchors Books 1988. Kindle.

6. Stanley, Andy. *Louder than Words: The Power of Uncompromised Living.* New York: WalterBrook Multnomah, 2004. Kindle. This comes from a retelling of a story about McCartney in Stanley's book.

www.ingramcontent.com/pod-product-compliance
Lightning Source LLC
Chambersburg PA
CBHW051724040426
42447CB00008B/971